I0416028

1000 Catcher in the Rye Facts

James Sampson

© Copyright 2020 James Sampson

All rights reserved.

Introduction

1000 Catcher in the Rye Facts contains all you could ever want to know about Salinger's timeless novel. Origins, trivia, themes, allusions, motifs, history, publication, covers, characters, vocabulary, slang, and much more.

(1) Jerome David Salinger was born in 1919 in New York.

(2) The Catcher in the Rye was published in 1951.

(3) Pencey Prep, the boarding school that Holden leaves at the start of the novel, is believed to be based on Valley Forge Military Academy. Salinger attended this institution in his youth. Pencey Prep (which is fictional) and Valley Forge Military Academy (which is real) are both in Pennsylvania.

(4) Holden says in The Catcher in the Rye that if a war breaks out he'll volunteer to sit on top of the atom bomb. This comment actually anticipates the end of Stanley Kubrick's classic film Dr Strangelove a decade later.

(5) It is alleged that Holden's first name might have been inspired by Holden Bowler - a man that Salinger knew in the army.

(6) A signed (by Salinger obviously) first edition of The Catcher in the Rye can sell for over $20,000.

(7) When Holden says he prefers that 'lunatic' in the Bible this is a reference to 'Legion' in Mark 5:5.

(8) The young prostitute Sunny in Catcher represents what Holden most fears. She has compromised with the world and allowed it to corrupt her.

(9) Salinger is said to have landed at Normandy on D-Day carrying six chapters of The Catcher in the Rye on him.

(10) When Salinger was at Valley Forge, a pupil named William Walters, who was bullied, fell off the roof of a dorm. Walters is the inspiration for James Castle in The Catcher in the Rye. Castle was a former schoolfriend of

Holden who jumped out of a window rather than retract calling a bully conceited.

(11) The prostitute Sunny says in the novel that Holden resembles the kid who fell off the boat. This is a reference to the 1937 movie Captains Courageous and its child actor star Freddie Bartholomew.

(12) Mr Antolini quotes Wilhelm Stekel to Holden. 'The mark of the immature man is that he wants to die nobly for a cause, while the mark of the mature man is that he wants to live humbly for one.' Wilhelm Stekel was an Austrian physician and psychologist. He was an early follower of Freud.

(13) The famous red carnival house cover used on the first hardback edition of The Catcher in the Rye was the creation of E. Michael Mitchell. Mitchell was a friend of Salinger and lived quite near him.

(14) Mitchell's red carnival horse illustration is rife with symbolism. The pole could be interpreted as Holden's desire to 'impale' himself to childhood.

(15) The term 'flit' is used by Holden Caulfield in the novel. Flit is period slang for someone who might be homosexual.

(16) The Pennsylvania Station that Holden uses in the novel was demolished in 1963.

(17) Benedict Arnold was a notorious traitor in the Revolutionary War.

(18) The Catcher in the Rye is called Il giovane Holden in Italy. This means The Young Holden.

(19) Holden losing the school fencing equipment on the

subway is something that also happened to JD Salinger when he was at school.

(20) JD Salinger took a trip overseas when The Catcher in the Rye was about to be published in America. He wanted to avoid the reviews and publicity.

(21) The Catcher in the Rye seems to attract a lot of bizarre conspiracy theories. One book even claimed that the novel was all about Freemasonry.

(22) The novel begins with Holden on top of a hill. This represents his sense of detachment from life.

(23) JD Salinger hated his photograph appearing on the dust jacket of early editions of The Catcher in the Rye. He had his photograph removed from future editions.

(24) Mitchell's famous carnival horse cover seems to be inspired by James Earle Fraser's sculpture The End of the Trail.

(25) Agerstown is not a real place and purely fictional.

(26) 'Galoshes' is a name for waterproof boots.

(27) The Catcher in the Rye was so ahead of its time it predated the start of the Beat Generation by six years.

(28) In chapter eighteen, Holden describes a film ('It was about this English guy, Alec something, that was in the war and loses his memory in the hospital and all...') but doesn't tell us the name of the film. The best guess is that Holden is talking about the 1942 film Random Harvest.

(29) One of Salinger's strictest stipulations for publishing The Catcher in the Rye was that on no account should the

publisher ever forward him any reviews · even if they were positive.

(30) Holden's recovery begins at the end of the novel when Phoebe makes Holden choose between her and the memory of his late brother Allie. She forces Holden to choose the land of the living.

(31) Salinger originally had six Caulfield stories written in the third person. These formed the basis for what would become The Catcher in the Rye.

(32) After he had finished writing The Catcher in the Rye, Salinger read out the entire book aloud to the New Yorker editor.

(33) Holden's immaturity is apparent in the way that he is a mass of contradictions. Holden refers to other people as phoney but also admits that he is a 'terrific' liar himself.

(34) There was a cadet named Ackley at Valley Forge when Salinger was there. One almost hopes the real life Ackley never read Catcher!

(35) One of the early Signet covers for the novel depicted Holden on the cover with a suitcase. This illustration was by James Avati. JD Salinger loathed this cover. Salinger liked his books to have blank covers with just text.

(36) Salinger had something in common with Holden in that he was also once expelled from a boarding school because of failing grades.

(37) The Seton Hotel is a real place.

(38) There are a number of references to 'highballs' in The Catcher in the Rye. This is a cocktail mixture · traditionally

composed of scotch & soda.

(39) Salinger used the early Caulfield stories to refine the character to the point where he was confident enough to write The Catcher in the Rye.

(40) After the death of Salinger in 2010, the JD Salinger Literary Trust said they would respect his wishes and not give the film or TV rights to the novel to anyone.

(41) Salinger wrote the words on the dust jacket in early editions of Catcher. He appears to struggle somewhat though to provide a coherent short summery of his own novel!

(42) The word 'chrissake' is used 31 times in The Catcher in the Rye.

(43) When he was in Europe during World War 2, a photograph was taken of Salinger writing at a desk. This is believed to be the only photograph in existence of him working on what became The Catcher in the Rye.

(44) A YouGov survey found that 52% of readers read Catcher because it was assigned reading. 27% of readers chose to read the book voluntarily for pleasure.

(45) The Catcher in the Rye was published as a digital ebook for the first time in 2019.

(46) The Star Tribune gave Catcher a very positive review when it came out in 1951. 'Despite your hoots of laughter at Holden's indomitable speech, this is in essence the tragic story of a problem child, unless indeed it's an indictment of a problem world. Month in, month out, novels don't come much better.'

(47) JD Salinger refused to do any publicity when The Catcher in the Rye was published.

(48) JD Salinger planned to release The Catcher in the Rye as a short novella at one point. He wasn't sure if he could make it work as a novel.

(49) Holden's parents live at 71st and Fifth Avenue near Central Park.

(50) There has, believe it or not, been an academic theory that Holden is narrating his tale in The Catcher in the Rye to an imaginary friend.

(51) The word 'grippe' is used at the start of the novel. This refers to influenza.

(52) Holden's red hunting hat is symbolic of his confusion about adulthood. The hat adds a childlike nature to his appearance - despite his height and early grey hairs.

(53) It has been speculated that Salinger got the name Holden Caulfield after looking at a film poster which bore the names Joan Caufield and William Holden. It was Joyce Maynard who claimed Salinger told her this.

(54) The first story that Salinger wrote featuring Holden Caulfield was called I'm Crazy.

(55) Holden is critical of the actor Laurence Olivier in The Catcher in the Rye. After the book was published, Salinger was mortified to bump into Olivier at a party in London.

(56) Salinger is said to have written a letter Laurence Olivier in which he said that he did not share Holden's opinion. In the book, Holden Caulfied is dismissive of Oliver's performance in a play.

(57) Not long after The Catcher in the Rye was published, Salinger moved to Cornish, New Hampshire, and stayed there for the rest of his life. This was his rural refuge from the fame that Catcher have given him.

(58) Don Hahn claims that Disney once planned to do a thinly veiled film version of The Catcher in the Rye featuring dogs! "Michael [Eisner] loved Catcher in the Rye and he said, 'We ought to do Catcher in the Rye.' And we told him the truth, which is [JD] Salinger's never going to do Catcher in the Rye for anybody. And he said, 'Well, let's just do that kind of story, that kind of growing up, coming of age story.' So it was that. Catcher in the Rye with German shepherds. I'm not making that up."

(59) There are themes of social class in Catcher. Holden tends to find the more educated and wealthy people he meets in the novel pretentious. There is a sharp contrast too between the swanky apartment of Mr Antolini and the dusty den of Mr Spencer. Antolini and Spencer are both in the same profession but they clearly live in completely different worlds.

(60) Holden's informal use of language in the novel is designed to make him feel more like a real person. It also helps the reader to identify with him more.

(61) A 2013 survey found that 34% of American adults had read The Catcher in the Rye.

(62) The Catcher in the Rye is one of the most banned books in American history.

(63) The Catcher in the Rye is translated into over thirty languages.

(64) Holden can't face meeting Jane Gallagher again because she might have changed or grown-up too much. He prefers the memory of her to the real thing.

(65) One of the main themes in The Catcher in the Rye is the loss of innocence.

(66) Holden mentions that a dessert called a Brown Betty is on the menu at Pencey Prep but that no one (apart from Ackley) eats it. A Brown Betty is a dessert made from fruit and sweetened crumbs. It is similar to a cobbler.

(67) The Edmont Hotel is fictional.

(68) The horse carnival carousel at Central Park is still there today. It dates back to 1871.

(69) The animator Ralph Bakshi wanted to make a Catcher in the Rye film. The chances of Salinger consenting to this were zero.

(70) Although Holden cherishes innocence, he is drawn to the adult world of bars, sleazy hotels, and prostitutes. This represents the struggle inside Holden to find his place in the world. He is torn between memory and experience.

(71) Little Shirley Beans is not a real song.

(72) Estelle Fletcher was a real person though. She was a Brunanter singer famous in the 1950s.

(73) In 1980, Mark David Chapman shot the singer John Lennon dead in New York and then sat calmly reading The Catcher in the Rye while he waited for the police to arrive.

(74) Mark David Chapman tried to use The Catcher in the Rye as a defence for why he had shot John Lennon.

Chapman said he identified with Holden and thought that John Lennon had become a phony. Chapman was obviously a man with mental health problems. This had tragic consequences.

(75) In 1981, John W Hinckley Jr shot President Ronald Reagan. The police found a copy of The Catcher in the Rye in Hinckley's hotel room after they arrested him. The incidents with Chapman and Hinckley were a dark and unwelcome connection to The Catcher in the Rye and Salinger. It must be stressed though that these men were clearly disturbed. They probably would have done something stupid and dangerous even if The Catcher in the Rye didn't exist. Hinckley had spent the previous years stalking the actress Jodie Foster because he was obsessed with the film Taxi Driver. No one would blame Martin Scorsese for Hinckley's crimes so it seems unfair to blame Salinger or Holden Caulfield.

(76) John W Hinckley had other books apart from The Catcher in the Rye in his hotel. Thanks to Chapman though, any dark link to The Catcher in the Rye was now scrutinised beyond reason and exaggerated.

(77) In 1989, the actress Rebecca Schaeffer resided in the Fairfax District of Los Angeles and had an apartment in a Mock Tudor house. One day, Schaeffer heard her doorbell and rushed down thinking it was a script she was expecting to be delivered that day. Instead she found a young man outside the house who turned out to be a fan who had tracked her down. She signed an autograph for him and then he left. Later in the afternoon, the young man returned and rang Schaeffer's bell again. This time, Rebecca Schaeffer was more short with him. She told the young man that he was wasting her precious time with these interruptions and that he should leave her alone. At this, the young man produced a gun and shot Schaeffer in

the chest. She was taken to hospital but dead within an hour. The young man who had killed Rebecca Schaeffer was 19 year-old Robert John Bardo. Bardo had become obsessed with Rebecca Schaeffer and once even tried to get onto the set of her sitcom My Sister Sam. It was reported that Bardo, like Chapman and Hinckley, was obsessed with The Catcher in the Rye. The evidence for this is vague. He owned a copy but then hundreds of millions of people own a copy of Catcher and have never killed anyone. Bardo's motivation for the murder was his anger that Schaeffer had done a love scene in the film Scenes from the Class Struggle in Beverly Hills. The murder had nothing at all to do with Holden Caulfield or Salinger.

(78) The word 'crumby' in Catcher in the Rye means shabby or disappointing.

(79) In 2020, Far out Magazine reported that Bob Dylan was approached to play Holden Caulfield in a proposed 1961 film version of Catcher. This story seems dubious at best as no one actually had permission to make a Catcher in the Rye movie.

(80) One of the reasons why Catcher became a cult book is that it came out as teenagers emerged as a distinct social group for the first time.

(81) Some parent and religious groups have complained that The Catcher in the Rye promotes occultism. It is genuinely baffling how they came to this conclusion.

(82) An important theme in The Catcher in the Rye is the superficial nature of adults. Holden thinks that most adults he meets are complete frauds.

(83) Salinger's parents lived in an apartment near Central Park. Salinger was therefore able to use his own extensive

knowledge of New York in the novel.

(84) The publisher Eugene Reynal rejected The Catcher in the Rye because he didn't like Holden Caulfield. This was obviously a very big mistake by Reynal.

(85) Believe it or not, The Catcher in the Rye was very popular in the Soviet Union.

(86) The novel's title is inspired by a Robert Burns poem.

(87) Holden' misquotes the Burns poem and by replacing Gin a body meet a body with When a body catch a body.

(88) The Catcher in the Rye was so popular that in no time at all it had to be reprinted five times after its release.

(89) Salinger served in the 12th US Infantry Regiment of the 4th Infantry Division in World War 2. He worked on some of what would eventually become The Catcher in the Rye during the war. Salinger landed at Normandy on D-Day and was there when the concentration camp at Dachau was liberated.

(90) In a letter to Ernest Hemingway, Salinger once suggested he could play the part of Holden Caulfield on the stage himself. It's hard to tell if he was joking but Salinger did want to be an actor when he was younger and loved the stage.

(91) Salinger is believed to have written most of the completed novel at a small rented house in Westport and in a Manhattan apartment.

(92) The Catcher in the Rye is definitely a 'marmite' book. People seem to either love it or hate it.

(93) Holden carries a lot of guilt in the novel because his younger brother Allie died of leukemia. Salinger lost many friends and comrades in the war and so one could suggest that Holden feels the same way that Salinger did in real life.

(94) Although they are mentioned, Holden's parents never actually appear in the novel.

(95) Holden is intentionally a character with many contradictions. He dislikes the adult world for its phoniness but he finds many people his own age also lack sincerity.

(96) It has been speculated that Holden's name has a deliberate subtext in that it sounds like 'hold-on'.

(97) Holden wants to stop children in a giant field of rye from falling from the edge of the field. This represents his desire to stop children from growing-up and becoming adults.

(98) Harcourt were supposed to publish the novel but they didn't really understand it. Salinger was frustrated by this and went to Little, Brown publishers instead.

(99) It is calculated that more than one hundred million people have read The Catcher in the Rye.

(100) The rock band Green Day had a song called Who Wrote Holden Caulfield?

(101) The red hunting hat that Holden wears is symbolic of his connection to his red-haired siblings Allie and Phoebe.

(102) Holden uses the word 'phony' 35 times in The Catcher in the Rye.

(103) Few people have experienced overnight fame in the way that Salinger did. One minute he was an obscure writer and the next minute he was the most talked about writer in America.

(104) The actor John Cusack said that, when he was young, it was always his dream to play Holden Caulfield.

(105) Salinger said of the photograph of him on the early Catcher editions dust jacket - 'Let's say I'm getting good and sick of bumping into that blown-up photograph of my face on the back of the dust jacket. I look forward to the day when I see it flapping against a lamp post, in a cold, wet Lexington Avenue wind.'

(106) Harcourt were so confused by The Catcher in the Rye they gave it to their school division to read. They didn't seem to know if the book was pitched at children or adults - which seems remarkable.

(107) The first hardback edition of The Catcher in the Rye was priced at three dollars.

(108) By the 1960s, The Catcher in the Rye was taught at around 280 colleges.

(109) Salinger had a verbal 'handshake' agreement with Robert Giroux at Harcourt to publish the book. Giroux was mortified when his boss Eugene Reynal disliked the book.

(110) Harcourt actually asked Salinger to rewrite The Catcher in the Rye. Salinger was never going to agree to this.

(111) Eugene Reynal asked if Holden was crazy when he met Salinger. Salinger was upset by this because he identified with Holden and had put a lot of himself into his

central character.

(112) Harcourt made another colossal blunder a few years later when they missed out on the chance to publish On the Road by Jack Kerouac. They asked Kerouac to rewrite the book and Kerouac (like Salinger) simply took his book somewhere else.

(113) Salinger asked Little, Brown (his publisher) not to send out advance copies of The Catcher in the Rye because he didn't want any publicity. The publishers were completely bemused by this eccentric request.

(114) Holden uses the word 'crazy' 35 times in The Catcher in the Rye.

(115) Holden purchases tickets to see the Lunts in The Catcher in the Rye. Lunt and Fontanne were a husband-and-wife acting team who appeared together in more than two dozen theatrical productions. Their plays included Arms and the Man (1925), The Goat Song (1926), The Doctor's Dilemma (1927), Elizabeth the Queen (1930), Idiot's Delight (1936), Amphitryon 38 (1938), and The Pirate (1942). The Lunts also appeared in films and on television.

(116) An early British edition of The Catcher in the Rye had a cover by Fritz Wegner. It featured Phoebe heading towards the carousel as Holden looks on.

(117) One of the British first editions with the Fritz Wegner cover can fetch $3000 in online auctions.

(118) Holden Caulfield's tipple of choice is Scotch & Soda.

(119) Holden remembers how Jane Gallagher, when playing checkers, would leave her kings at the back of the

board and refuse to move them. This eccentric custom of Jane is how Holden approaches life. He can't seem to engage or move forward. Holden also wants to keep his image of Jane trapped and stationary - just like her kings in checkers.

(120) Holden has a Malted when he meets the nuns. Malted milk was popular at soda shops in the 1950s.

(121) In 1976, a legislative hearing in Oklahoma City had to deal with a case where a group of Catcher protesters wanted to stop a bookseller from selling the book. The protest group picketed the hearing to drum up publicity. It sounds absolutely ridiculous today that people were trying to get a book banned.

(122) Despite protests against alleged communist themes, The Catcher in the Rye is a rather apolitical book.

(123) Holden has a fantasy in the novel of running away and living in a remote cabin. Salinger did this himself in real life. Holden's fantasy clearly expressed Salinger's own desire for privacy and peace.

(124) Holden calls himself a 'sort of an atheist' in The Catcher in the Rye. This line is one of (the many) reasons why religious groups were up in arms over the book.

(125) In 1949, a film called My Foolish Heart adapted Salinger's 1948 short story Uncle Wiggily in Connecticut. Salinger absolutely despised this film when he saw it. My Foolish Heart probably explains why Salinger would never let anyone make a Catcher in the Rye film.

(126) Despite his refusal to allow anyone to film Catcher and barbs at Hollywood in the book, Salinger was a huge film buff and had a projector at his house to run movies.

(127) Young readers in Eastern Europe seemed to respond to The Catcher in the Rye in a profound and personal way when they encountered it during the Cold War. The theme of Holden as a rebel who didn't approve of the system he was part of obviously had some resonance for those growing-up under the Iron Curtain.

(128) The New York Times gave The Catcher in the Rye a positive review when it was first published.

(129) The actor Edward Norton said that The Catcher in the Rye was his favourite novel.

(130) The New Yorker declined to publish excerpts from The Catcher in the Rye because the editors didn't care for the book much. They thought Holden was improbably articulate for a teenager and lacked credibility as a character. Salinger was quite hurt by this.

(131) The Catcher in the Rye stayed on the New York Times bestseller list for seven months when it came out.

(132) Holden appears to be narrating The Catcher in the Rye from a hospital of some sort.

(133) Holden visits his old teacher Mr Antolini in the story but is spooked when he is woken up by Mr Antolini stroking his head. The actions of Mr Antolini are not explained by Salinger in the novel. Did he have a sexual motive or was he merely being kind? Those who believe that Catcher has a sexual abuse subtext might lean to the former. A more plausible theory is that Salinger is showing us that Holden has to learn to trust people more and not see only the bad things in life.

(134) Salinger described Holden Caulfield as a 'frozen

moment in time' and said there would be no more stories about him after Catcher.

(135) The Catcher in the Rye was the only novel that Salinger wrote. He saw himself primarily as a short story writer.

(136) When he declines to join Phoebe on the carousel at the end of the book, Holden has accepted that he must move on from childhood and the death of Allie.

(137) It has been alleged that The Catcher in the Rye is an MKUltra kill trigger. Project MKUltra is a top secret CIA funded experiment into mind control that made use of the mind-altering drug LSD. MKUltra was a response to American fears that the Soviets were more advanced in brainwashing and mind control techniques. The MKUltra experiments included remote viewing and extrasensory perception. While these things were never proven to be real, the actual experiments did actually happen. Project MKUltra ended in 1973 and only became public knowledge after the experiment was terminated. The attempts to connect Salinger to MKUltra were far-fetched to say the least.

(138) Holden loves the Museum of Natural History because nothing there seems to change. The exhibits are frozen in time. He wishes life was like this.

(139) In 1960, an Oklahoma teacher was removed from their position for choosing Catcher as a study subject for pupils.

(140) The James Avati early cover of The Catcher in the Rye had a blurb that said - "This unusual book may shock you, will make you laugh and may break your heart—but you will never forget it." You can only imagine the horror of

JD Salinger when he saw this.

(141) Salinger never posed for an official photograph again after posing for The Catcher in the Rye dust jacket. Although he lived into his nineties, Salinger was frozen in time as the 32 year-old man who had posed for the Catcher dust jacket photograph.

(142) The Russian translation of The Catcher in the Rye is Nad propastyu vo rzhi.

(143) A YouGov survey found that 61% of people who had read The Catcher in the Rye said it was an enjoyable experience.

(144) In the novel David Copperfield, the word 'caul' (an embryonic covering at birth) is used. This might have inspired Holden's second name.

(145) The Catcher in the Rye was first published in the Soviet Union in the November 1960 issue of literary magazine Inostrannaya Literatura.

(146) Red hunting hats are worn to make one safer. This could be why Holden finds it comforting to have one.

(147) DreamWorks studio head Jeffrey Katzenberg once tried to contact JD Salinger to ask if Steven Spielberg could have the rights to make a film based on the novel. Salinger's agents knew the author would decline this offer so they didn't even bother to pass Katzenberg's request onto him.

(149) In the 1950s, the Australian government was gifted some copies of The Catcher in the Rye by the American ambassador. However, the authorities in Australia confiscated the books because The Catcher in the Rye was

banned in Australia at the time.

(150) Holden uses the word 'goddam' 245 times in The Catcher in the Rye.

(151) When he was young, JD Salinger's girlfriend for a brief time was Oona O'Neill. Oona was the teenage daughter of playwright Eugene O'Neill. Salinger wanted to marry Oona but while he was in Europe during World War 2 she went to Hollywood and ended up marrying the much older Charlie Chaplin.

(152) Holden Caulfield doesn't seem to like Hollywood very much. This is alleged to be because of Salinger losing Oona O'Neill to Charlie Chaplin.

(153) The Catcher in the Rye became a cult book with students.

(154) JD Salinger enrolled at New York University in 1936 but didn't last very long.

(155) William Faulkner was a big fan of The Catcher in the Rye.

(156) Salinger had happy memories of Valley Forge Military Academy. He enjoyed it considerably more than Holden enjoyed Pencey Prep.

(157) Woody Allen said that The Catcher in the Rye is one of the few great works of fiction that he finds a pleasure to read (as opposed to hard work).

(158) In the 1930s, JD Salinger briefly worked for his father's potted meat and food business in Europe. Salinger escaped from Austria two week before Adolf Hitler annexed the country.

(159) Harvey Weinstein once tried to get the film rights to The Catcher in the Rye. As ever, Salinger wasn't interested in the slightest.

(160) JD Salinger went to Ursinus College in Collegeville, Pennsylvania.

(161) The Christian Science Monitor gave The Catcher in the Rye a crappy review when it came out. They called the language 'vulgar' and were shocked by the use of the f-word.

(162) Salinger really hated publishers and publishing. He was fortunate that Catcher gave him enough financial independence to publish on his own terms - or not at all.

(163) The Catcher in the Rye sold poorly in Britain when it was first released. Reader confusion at American slang was cited as a possible reason for this.

(164) Salinger was interested in Zen Buddhism. Zen teaches that one should detach oneself from ego. This is one explanation for why Salinger hated the fame that The Catcher in the Rye gave him.

(165) Salinger was so anhedonic he even disliked positive reviews.

(166) Salinger never published anything after 1965.

(167) The way Holden flips his red hunting hat from back to front is symbolic of his confusion over being trapped in limbo between childhood and adulthood.

(168) The actress Winona Ryder said The Catcher in the Rye is her favourite book.

(169) Holden seems to suggest that Jane Gallagher suffered sexual harassment or even abuse from her 'booze hound' stepfather.

(170) JD Salinger always told friends that he was very much like Holden Caulfield.

(171) Elia Kazan wanted to turn The Catcher in the Rye into a Broadway play in the early 1960s. Salinger would not consent to this though.

(172) Jean Miller, who as a teenager had a friendship and brief romance with Salinger before Catcher came out, said that Salinger was very nervous at how people would react to Holden's slang. Salinger feared they might find it confusing and unnecessary.

(173) Jean Miller said Salinger confessed to her that he didn't think he had another novel in him after completing The Catcher in the Rye.

(174) The short stories that feature Holden Caulfield date back to 1941.

(175) There is not continuity in the Holden Caulfield short stories and Holden isn't always the same character. Salinger even kills Holden off in one of them.

(176) The Catcher in the Rye can be interpreted as a PTSD novel inspired by Salinger's harrowing experiences in World War 2.

(177) Although Holden doesn't care much for Brown Betty, it was apparently a favorite dessert of President Ronald Reagan and First Lady Nancy Reagan. They often served it to guests at the White House.

(178) When the novel was published in Israel, the publishers wanted to change the title because Catcher in the Rye was impossible to translate into Hebrew. Salinger was predictably annoyed by this.

(179) The early editions of the novel with Salinger's photograph on the dust jacket are more valuable today than later editions.

(180) In 2009, a Swedish man named Fredrik Colting published an unauthorised sequel to The Catcher in the Rye. The book was called 60 Years Later: Coming Through the Rye and had a character named Mr C slipping out of a retirement home to go to New York. Colting used the name John David California on the book.

(181) Salinger's legal team sued 60 Years Later: Coming Through the Rye for copyright infringement. This stopped the book from being published in America.

(182) Of selling the film rights to Catcher, Salinger once said - 'I'll try to tell you what my attitude is to the stage and screen rights of The Catcher in the Rye. I've sung this tune quite a few times, so if my heart doesn't seem to be in it, try to be tolerant. Firstly, it is possible that one day the rights will be sold. Since there's an ever-looming possibility that I won't die rich, I toy very seriously with the idea of leaving the unsold rights to my wife and daughter as a kind of insurance policy. It pleasures me no end, though, I might quickly add, to know that I won't have to see the results of the transaction. I keep saying this and nobody seems to agree, but The Catcher in the Rye is a very novelistic novel. There are readymade "scenes" — only a fool would deny that — but, for me, the weight of the book is in the narrator's voice, the non-stop peculiarities of it, his personal, extremely discriminating attitude to his reader-listener, his

asides about gasoline rainbows in street puddles, his philosophy or way of looking at cowhide suitcases and empty toothpaste cartons – in a word, his thoughts. He can't legitimately be separated from his own first-person technique. True, if the separation is forcibly made, there is enough material left over for something called an Exciting (or maybe just Interesting) Evening in the Theater. But I find that idea if not odious, at least odious enough to keep me from selling the rights. There are many of his thoughts, of course, that could be laboured into dialogue – or into some sort of stream-of-consciousness loud-speaker device – but laboured is exactly the right word. What he thinks and does so naturally in his solitude in the novel, on the stage could at best only be pseudo-simulated, if there is such a word (and I hope not). Not to mention, God help us all, the immeasurably risky business of using actors. Have you ever seen a child actress sitting crosslegged on a bed and looking right? I'm sure not. And Holden Caulfield himself, in my undoubtedly super-biassed opinion, is essentially unactable. A Sensitive, Intelligent, Talented Young Actor in a Reversible Coat wouldn't nearly be enough. It would take someone with X to bring it off, and no very young man even if he has X quite knows what to do with it. And, I might add, I don't think any director can tell him. I'll stop there. I'm afraid I can only tell you, to end with, that I feel very firm about all this, if you haven't already guessed.'

(183) Salinger's short story The Boy in the People Shooting Hat was part of the basis for what later became The Catcher in the Rye. Salinger was devastated when the New Yorker rejected this story.

(184) The Catcher in the Rye was selected as the summer selection by the staff of Book of the Month Club in 1951. This was considered to be a big honour at the time.

(185) Salinger was aware that Catcher was controversial

and had attracted complaints from parent and religious groups. Salinger was very saddened by this. 'I'm aware that many of my friends will be saddened and shocked, or shock-saddened, over some of the chapters in The Catcher in the Rye,' wrote Salinger. 'Some of my best friends are children. In fact, all my best friends are children. It's almost unbearable for me to realize that my book will be kept on a shelf out of their reach.'

(186) A 'chiffonier' is a bureau with a mirror.

(187) After the publication of The Catcher in the Rye and its huge success, Salinger was invited to his old school Valley Forge to attend a dinner in his honour. Salinger didn't turn up. He came up with an excuse that he was going away on a trip.

(188) James Avatai said of his Catcher in the Rye cover art - "JD Salinger didn't like my cover for Catcher in the Rye. In fact, he resisted the very idea of having artwork on the cover. One day he came to the NAL offices to complain about it. We went together into a little room and I said, 'Come on! These guys are doing the selling, they know how to sell.' But he was very reluctant. At first, his idea was to have something less realistic, more the printmaker's look. But since that was impossible - he was not yet a known author - he wanted something more sentimental. The carousel in the park, you know. I didn't like that cover that I ended up painting too much myself. Not because of the idea, but it's not very well painted. But, anyway, I may be the only person who ever changed Salinger's mind."

(189) When the novel was translated into Swedish, most of the cuss and swear words were taken out.

(190) Bill Gates said The Catcher in the Rye was his favourite book.

(191) Holden's older brother D.B writes scripts in Hollywod. Holden would prefer him to write more short stories (like The Secret Goldfish). D.B (another character who is mentioned but never seen) is used by Salinger for some more barbs at Hollywood.

(192) There was a Scottish pop group who called themselves The Secret Goldfish.

(193) Jerry Lewis said he tried to get the film rights to The Catcher in the Rye in the 1970s.

(194) The Catcher in the Rye was a big influence on Sylvia Plath's The Bell Jar.

(195) In 1989, a small town in the Mojave Desert banned The Catcher in the Rye.

(196) Marlon Brando was among the many people in Hollywood who tried to obtain the rights to make a Catcher in the Rye movie.

(197) When Holden uses the term 'snowing' in the novel he means to charm or sweet-talk.

(198) A YouGov poll found that 75% of American readers first read The Catcher in the Rye when they were in high school.

(199) Sally Hayes in The Catcher in the Rye is alleged to be based on Oona O'Neill (or Oona Chaplin as she became).

(200) The word 'bastard' is used 58 times in The Catcher in the Rye.

(201) In the 1963 Penguin edition, the passage where

someone has scrawled 'f***' you on the wall of Phoebe's school was censored and the f-word removed. Later editions put the f-word back in.

(202) The book's Hebrew title means Me, New York, and Everything Else in English.

(203) Ward Stradlater, Holden's Pencey roommate, is one of the least pretentious and uncomplicated people Holden meets in the book. Stradlater is not sympathetic though. He is presented as vain and shallow and his attitude to girls leaves something to be desired.

(204) One could argue that Catcher offers a critique of capitalist industry society. Holden loves the idea of ducking out of the rat race and urban jungle altogether.

(205) Tobey Maguire is yet another Hollywood figure who made a doomed attempt to get the rights to make a Catcher in the Rye film.

(206) The Belle & Sebastian's song La Pastie de la Bourgeoisie is about The Catcher in the Rye.

(207) Holden's (dead) brother Allie and his childhood crush Jane Gallagher are two of the most vivid characters in The Catcher in the Rye and yet they don't appear in the novel. We only learn about them through Holden's narration and memories.

(208) There is though a substantial Jane Gallagher flashback in chapter eleven.

(209) When Holden says 'dough', he means money.

(210) Some scholars think that Salinger's obsession with Zen was a disaster for his writing. His work became

somewhat esoteric after Catcher.

(211) Salinger gives Holden his own physical characteristics. Both are tall and thin.

(212) The f-word appears six times in the novel.

(213) When Holden says he misses the people he knew at Pencey, even the students he didn't much like, this could be Salinger reflecting on his old army colleagues.

(214) When he moved to Cornish after Catcher was published, Salinger was friendly with the local students. He broke off contact though when one of them published his quotes for a student paper in a magazine as if he had submitted to a formal interview. Salinger felt as if his trust had been betrayed.

(215) In one of the Caulfield short stories, the character is a missing soldier.

(216) When Catcher was published, it was assumed that this would be merely the first of many famous novels by Salinger. This assumption was completely wrong.

(217) The Wes Anderson film Rushmore clearly owes something to The Catcher in the Rye.

(218) Holden dislikes the slobbish Ackley and finds him annoying. You could argue though that Holden and Ackley have a lot in common. They both refuse to compromise with life and are stubbornly individual.

(219) The snowball that Holden can't bring himself to let go of represents innocence and purity.

(220) The Catcher in the Rye took ten years to finish.

(221) In their original review of Catcher, the Chicago Daily Tribune said that the book 'largely succeeds'. This was hardly an enthusiastic review.

(222) In 1997, the parent of a Marysville High School student got Catcher pulled from the curriculum of her daughter's school. She said - "We live in America. You can like garbage. We just felt there had to be better books out there."

(223) Films as diverse as Rebel Without a Cause and Less Than Zero owe something to The Catcher in the Rye.

(224) Salinger worked for Counter Intelligence during and after the war. This is perhaps why he is sometimes linked to government MKUltra conspiracies.

(225) Salinger is rare in that he turned his back on fame at the height of his success.

(226) Salinger said he found the media attention from Catcher to be 'completely demoralizing'.

(227) Holden's grey hairs suggest that he is an old soul in a young body.

(228) In 1951, Salinger named Kafka, Flaubert, Tolstoy, Chekhov, Dostoevsky, Proust, O'Casey, Rilke, Lorca, Keats, Rimbaud, Burns, E.Bronte, Jane Austen, Henry James, Blake, and Coleridge as his favourite authors.

(229) Those who encountered Salinger around the time that Catcher was published found him to be surprisingly shy and quiet. He seemed shellshocked by his fame.

(230) Mark Chapman later said that The Catcher in the

Rye had not made him shoot John Lennon. Chapman has been denied parole eleven times and remains in prison.

(231) Mark Chapman said he wrote a letter of apology to Salinger from prison. It is unknown if Salinger ever received the letter.

(232) Salinger never made any comments about Mark Chapman or John Hinckley Jr. Salinger read newspapers and had a TV set though so must have been aware of them.

(233) A woman in Cornish, who vaguely knew Salinger, said that after John Lennon was shot she saw Salinger in the street looking glum and distracted. Salinger would usually say hello to her but he seemed to be in a world of his own that week.

(234) John Hinckley Jr was released on parole in 2016.

(235) Salinger was sometimes called a recluse. This is not accurate. Salinger had friends and was fond of travel. He simply stopped giving interviews.

(236) If one believes that Mr Antolini had an unsavoury sexual interest in Holden, then the passage involving him waking Holden up could be read as Salinger telling us that danger and corruption (if you can call it that) comes in all guises - even swanky Manhattan apartments. The consensus on this passage is far from universal though.

(237) When Holden says 'louse' he means someone who is dishonest or dodgy.

(238) Holden has lost his own innocence in The Catcher in the Rye because of the death of his brother Allie.

(239) The Catcher in the Rye can be read as a meditation

on the random and unavoidable nature of death.

(240) When Holden says 'rubberneck' this means to stare at someone or something.

(241) The main source of Holden's depression is that he can never live up to the innocence and purity of the memory of his late brother Allie.

(242) Holden has to learn that living up to his memory of Allie is impossible.

(243) Holden's refusal to give Sunny and Maurice the extra five dollars represents his refusal to compromise with the world as it is.

(244) Sally Hayes featured in the short story Slight Rebellion off Madison.

(245) When Holden says 'crumb-bum' he means someone who is lazy and slobby.

(246) Holden donates $10 to the nuns he meets at the station. In contrast to Maurice and Sunny (who represent corruption and lost innocence), the nuns represent goodness and sincerity.

(247) The nuns at the station give Holden hope. They show that one can live an adult life without become corrupt or phony.

(248) Salinger said that publishing a book was embarrassing. He likened it to 'walking down Madison avenue with your pants down'.

(249) Salinger shortened his name to JD Salinger because he didn't want to be confused with a writer named Jerome

Faith Baldwin.

(250) In the 1940s, Salinger seriously considered writing a Catcher in the Rye play for the stage.

(251) Jack Nicholson is another person who made a futile effort to get the Catcher movie rights.

(252) There is a story that when Elia Kazan was trying to get the stage rights to Catcher, he went to see Salinger and had the door shut on him after he explained who he was. This might be apocryphal.

(253) Salinger once said that child actor (of the era) Margaret O'Brien would be his choice to play Phoebe in a Catcher stage play.

(254) The short story I'm Crazy is very similar to Catcher. In this story Holden is expelled from school.

(255) Holden's idiom 'shot the breeze' means to make small talk.

(256) In the short story Slight Rebellion off Madison, Holden's middle name is Morrisey.

(257) Those who knew Salinger when he was writing Catcher in Westport, say that he had many doubts about the novel. He had no idea if a story about a teenage boy would work or have any appeal.

(258) When Holden says someone 'kills him' he means that they have delighted or amused him in some way. It can also mean they have surprised him.

(259) When they rejected The Catcher in the Rye, the New York Times said they simply didn't believe that one family

(the Caulfields) would have four such 'extraordinary' children.

(260) 'Goose' means to flick someone or snap at them with a towel.

(261) When Holden says 'horse around' this means to mess around or lightly canoodle.

(262) Ernest Jones in The Nation gave one of the most withering reviews of Catcher when it came out in 1951. 'Echoes reach me of the popularity of The Catcher in the Rye. Why has this unpretentious, mildly affecting chronicle of a few days in the life of a disturbed adolescent been read with enthusiasm by Book-of-the-Month Club and lending-library adults ordinarily concerned with fiction as a frivolous diversion or as a source of lofty, incontrovertible platitudes? Entirely, I think, because, like many contemporary and highly praised novels written on the assumption that the mere record of budding sensitiveness automatically results in fiction, the book is a mirror. It reflects something not at all rich and strange but what every sensitive sixteen-year-old since Rousseau has felt, and of course what each one of us is certain he has felt. The skill with which all this has been worked into 277 pages is most ingenious. But as it proceeds on its insights, which are not really insights since they are so general, The Catcher in the Rye becomes more and more a case history of all of us. Radically this writing depends on the reader's recollection of merely similar difficulties; the unique crisis and the unique anguish are not re-created. These emotional ups and downs become increasingly factitious—so much must be included to elicit memories of so many callow heartbreaks—and though always lively in its parts, the book as a whole is predictable and boring.'

(263) The words 'sort of' are used 109 times in the novel.

(264) The reader desperately wants Holden to meet up with Jane Gallagher again but Salinger refuses to give us this moment. We are left to wonder if Jane would have been a disappointment to Holden and changed beyond recognition or if she might be essentially the same (though of course older) and a great tonic to him.

(265) It is not known if The Secret Goldfish was a story idea that Salinger once considered for himself or simply something he made up for Catcher.

(266) Holden claims to be illiterate but clearly loves books and reading. This is another contradiction in the character.

(267) The Catcher in the Rye is called Bjargvætturinn í grasinu in Iceland. The rough translation is Saviour in the Grass.

(268) When Holden says 'can' he means the bathroom or toilet.

(269) There are 73,921 words in The Catcher in the Rye.

(270) Phoebe's name is used 116 times in The Catcher in the Rye.

(271) The word 'mushy' in Catcher means maudlin or depressed.

(272) Holden's concern about the ducks represents fears for himself.

(273) The Catcher in the Rye is called Çavdar Tarlasında Çocuklar in Turkey. This means Kids in the Rye Field.

(274) Ernie's Bar is fictional.

(275) The Mel Gibson film Conspiracy Theory has a plot about brainwashed assassins that involves The Catcher in the Rye.

(276) The Catcher in the Rye is called Raddaren I Noden in Sweden.

(277) Rockefeller Center Ice Rink, where Holden and Sally go, is of course a real place.

(278) Holden appears to be suffering from a bipolar disorder. His ability to make rational decisions is impaired and he suffers mood swings.

(279) Holden wears his cap back to front because it makes him look like a 'catcher' in baseball.

(280) The Edmont Hotel is believed to have been based on the New Yorker Hotel.

(281) When Holden says 'give her the time' this seems to be an idiom for sexual contact.

(282) Holden passes on the Pencey Prep steak and buys a burger later. We gather from Holden that a steak at Pencey is cheap and almost inedible. They only serve them so that boys will tell their parents they get served steak at the school. This makes the school 'phony' to Holden.

(283) 'Grools' means ugly.

(284) The Wicker Bar is in the Seton Hotel. The Seton Hotel doesn't have a bar but they still get visits from Catcher in the Rye fans who presume they have one.

(285) The Catcher in the Rye is called L'Attrape-cœurs in

France. This means The Heart Catcher.

(286) Mark Twain used colloquial language in The Adventures of Huckleberry Finn. The Catcher in the Rye follows in that tradition.

(287) Holden seems to have little interest in food much of the time. He orders some doughnuts at one point but can't eat them. He does though have a breakfast of orange juice, bacon and eggs, toast and coffee. Holden says that normally he would just have juice for breakfast.

(288) The Museum of Natural history in New York has over 34 million artifacts.

(289) When Holden adds the word 'old' before someone's name this is often (though not always) a term of endearment.

(290) Although he was named Jerome, Salinger's friends and family always called him Sonny or Jerry.

(291) 'Buzz' means to telephone someone.

(292) The Catcher in the Rye was said to be especially difficult to translate into German.

(293) Phoebe's middle name is Josephine.

(294) The reference to David Copperfield at the start of Catcher is no coincidence. Catcher, like David Copperfield, is a journey through the adult world from the perspective of a young person.

(295) The Catcher in the Rye is called De vanger in het graan in Holland. The translation is The Catcher in the Grain.

(296) The short stories that were used heavily by Salinger for The Catcher in the Rye are This Sandwich has no Mayonnaise, I'm Crazy, An Ocean Full of Bowling Balls, The Last and Best of the Peter Pans, Slight Rebellion Off Madison.

(297) Believe it or not, despite his morose reputation, Salinger was fond of dancing in his youth. He includes some dancing scenes in Catcher.

(298) It is said that the pages of Catcher in the Rye that Salinger carried during World War 2 were like an amulet to him. He felt like they gave him a reason to survive the war.

(299) Salinger is alleged to have said that he sometimes wished he hadn't written The Catcher in the Rye. The fame it brought him was hard to cope with.

(300) The Catcher in the Rye is critical of the education system and boarding schools and yet Salinger sent his daughter Margaret away to a boarding school.

(301) Salinger was obsessive about total control of the publishing process. It was very painful for him at the start when he had to compromise on the early cover designs and release strategy of Catcher.

(302) Salinger did not use the names of real hotels all the time in Catcher for obvious reasons. A real hotel would not take too kindly to be being depicted as 'lousy with perverts' or a place where pimps and prostitutes ply their trade.

(303) Salinger's friend Peter De Vries suggested that he should come up with a better and more 'catchy' title for The Catcher in the Rye. Salinger, wisely, declined to do this.

(304) When he was writing Catcher, Salinger would refer to it as the prep school boy book.

(305) When they rejected Catcher, the New Yorker wrote Salinger a letter in which they said they found the novel too 'ingenious and ingrown'. They felt the book was too self-conscious and not natural.

(306) The great irony is that the New Yorker gave Catcher a glowing review when it came out and said it was a brilliant novel. They were rather embarrassed that they had rejected the chance to publish extracts.

(307) Salinger experienced more than his fair share of rejection before Catcher came out.

(308) Gore Vidal was a big fan of The Catcher in the Rye and championed the book on its release.

(309) Salinger allowed a short biography of himself to appear on the dust jacket of the first editions. The bio didn't say much. It merely said that Salinger had written stories since he was 15 and served in the army.

(310) Salinger said that biographies of writers never interested him · least of all one about himself.

(311) Those who call The Catcher in the Rye gloomy or depressing seem to overlook the fact that the book is full of deadpan sarcastic humour and often very funny.

(312) The perception that Holden is a proxy for Salinger was unavoidable. Salinger has Holden haunt the New York stomping ground that Salinger knew so well himself.

(313) When he moved to Cornish after Catcher came out, Salinger built a woodland bunker to write in. It is said that

even his family rarely saw him.

(314) Salinger really hated literary prizes. He liked writing but hated everything that came with it.

(315) Bantam's 1964 cover for Catcher was designed by Salinger. He chose the font and cover colour.

(316) Holden's antipathy to Sally is because she represents convention. Sally is more sensible and mature than Holden and gives him a glimpse at the type of conformity he is not ready for.

(317) Holden becomes an adult on his own terms at the end of Catcher. He becomes an adult for the sake of Phoebe.

(318) Phoebe decides she will run away with Holden at the end of Catcher. Holden tells her she can't. Phoebe is shrewd because her actions force Holden to come to his senses and · finally · act like an adult.

(319) By the end of The Catcher in the Rye, Holden has realised that he can't live his life trying to live up to his dead brother. He realises that he needs to have more consideration for his living sister.

(320) The record Little Shirley Beans, which Holden drops and breaks, is a symbol of how one can not live in the past.

(321) In moments of despair, Holden speaks to his dead brother Allie. This illustrates the lack of adult guidance in his life.

(322) The tension between fantasy and reality is very apparent in Holden. He is prone to flights of fantasy.

(323) Holden's trip to New York is a desperate attempt to

stave off reality and impending adulthood · two things Holden knows that he can't avoid forever.

(324) Holden is fearful of adulthood because he believes it might sever his connection to his late brother Allie.

(325) The contradictions in Holden's character make him more realistic and believable.

(326) Catcher was ahead of its time so one can see why it might have been controversial to a minority in the 1950s. It is baffling though why people were still trying to ban the book fifty years later.

(327) Salinger is inconsistent when it comes to Holden's appearance. Holden tells us he is tall with some grey hairs and yet Sunny says he looks like a famous child actor!

(328) It is ironic that Holden says when you read a good book you feel like phoning the author. That would have been impossible for anyone who enjoyed The Catcher in the Rye!

(329) Fans of Catcher seem to think it was probably for the best that a film was never made.

(330) Holden has a fear of the sexual world of adulthood but is attracted to it also. This creates confusion and tension.

(331) Salinger never wrote any more Holden Caulfield stories after Catcher.

(332) The incidents involving Mark Chapman and others were unfortunate and unfair because Catcher does not advocate violence. Holden is so gentle he worries about the ducks in winter!

(333) Holden's lack of street smarts is evident when he asks his cab driver to come for a drink. Holden has let a stranger know that he is alone in the city with money.

(334) Holden is clearly suffering from survivor guilt after the death of Alie. This is something Salinger should have experienced himself after the war.

(335) Holden's parents don't feature in Catcher because Holden is doing his best to avoid them. This is a clever plot device because it makes Holden feel more disconnected.

(336) Salinger is said to have disliked the Beat Generation that followed in Catcher's wake. Salinger did not approve of their use of drugs and their lifestyles.

(337) Letters signed by JD Salinger can sell for between $4,000 to $10,000 online.

(338) Ernie's is in Greenwich Village on the west side of Lower Manhattan.

(339) You could argue that Holden does become a 'catcher' in the end because he will be Phoebe's guardian in the last years of her childhood.

(340) Sunny takes the extra $5 from Holden while he is being roughed up by Maurice. Salinger seems to imply that Sunny, while corrupted, is not all bad. By taking the money herself, Sunny saves Holden from further harm.

(341) Holden's misreading of the Burns poem is very important. The lines Holden gets wrong said 'meet a body'. That is Holden's problem in a nutshell. He is making things worse for himself by (impossibly) trying to 'catch' people rather than actually 'meet' them.

(342) Ossenburger is a former pupil at Pencey who set a
funeral business and became wealthy. He has a wing at the
school named after him because he donated money to
Pencey. Ossenburger returned to the school to give a speech
and Holden hated having to sit through it. Ossenburger is a
big crooked phony according to Holden. Holden's distaste
for Ossenburger has a deeper subtext though. Holden is
bitter and angry that death took Allie away and
Ossenburger has become wealthy through a business that
profits from death.

(343) Holden admires Selma Thurmer - the daughter of the
headmaster at Pencey Prep. Selma never took her father
being headmaster as a big deal or pretended he was an
especially inspiring man. Holden admired the fact that
Selma was very honest and not pretentious. She was not a
phony.

(344) Salinger experienced the Battle of Hürtgen Forest in
the war. The Battle of Hürtgen Forest was a fight for a
wooded area on the Belgian-Germany border fought by
Americans and Germans. It was a bloody and tough battle.
The Germans lost but managed to hold up the Allied
advance for six months in this specific area. 30,000
American soldiers were killed or wounded in this battle.

(345) It could be that Holden wishes he was like Ward
Stradlater. Stradlater, unlike Holden, doesn't think about
things too much - and so will be less prone to introspection
or depression. Stradlater is also more sexually experienced
than Holden.

(346) Carl Luce was Holden's old school advisor. When he
meets up with him, Luce advises that Holden should
consult a psychologist. Carl Luce is not presented in a
sympathetic way (he comes across as a dreadful snob in the
book) but Salinger gives Luce genuine wisdom because his

advice is probably the best that anyone offers Holden in the story.

(347) Horwitz, the cab-driver, tells Holden that Mother Nature will take care of the fish in the winter. Horwitz, in his grouchy and slightly unwitting sort of way, is actually delivering a message of reassurance to Holden.

(348) Bernice, Marty, and Laverne, the three women that Holden encounters in the nightclub of the Edmont Hotel, are used by Salinger to illustrate the superficial and shallow nature of people. The women hardly take in a word Holden says and are desperate to see a famous person in the club.

(349) When Holden calls Maurice a 'chiseling moron', chiseling obviously means 'cheating'.

(350) Holden seems to be on a quest to find a simpler way of life outside the system. Salinger was on this quest too in his private life.

(351) Bernice, Marty, and Laverne illustrate how alone Holden feels and how difficult it is to make a connection.

(352) Carl Luce seems to find Holden a dreadful bore when they meet up. Salinger uses this scene to show us that Holden is not very mature for his age. Carl Luce finds Holden childish and tiresome.

(353) Phoebe represents the sincerity that Holden can't always find evidence of in the adult world.

(354) Salinger seems to suggest that Ward Stradlater is the sort of person the 'system' favours. Stradlater has a big ego and, although easygoing, if push came to shove would probably not be constricted by a moral compass to get what

he wanted.

(355) The death of Allie has made it difficult for Holden to connect to other people. He is frightened that they might be taken away from him like Allie was.

(356) Holden conjures Allie in his imagination as a way of keeping a connection to him. If he talks to Allie it makes him feel as if Allie is not really gone.

(357) Holden thinks that he is is less intelligent and kind than Allie was. This why he still feels so much guilt and sorrow at Allie's death.

(358) Holden's desire to be a catcher in a field of rye and holding back time to keep children innocent is a completely impossible dream. Holden's arc will only be completed when he comes to accept this.

(359) In the 1960s, The Catcher in the Rye was taught on the curriculum of some private schools in the Soviet Union.

(360) The American writers Museum wrote that E. Michael Mitchell's cover is a perfect illustration because it suggests Holden is 'still bound to the carousel horse of childhood'.

(361) Salinger's early novella version of Catcher was about 90 pages long.

(362) Judith Guest's Ordinary People is one of many novels clearly inspired by The Catcher in the Rye.

(363) There is a reference to a beverage called a 'Tom Collins' in Catcher. This beverage consists of soda water, gin, lemon juice, and sugar.

(364) Holden seems to be fond of Canasta. This is a card

game.

(365) In 1949, Salinger said in an interview - "I've written biographical notes for a few magazines, and I doubt if I ever said anything honest in them."

(366) Salinger was said to enjoy scotch and soda - just like Holden does in the book.

(367) Holden seems to like pinball. The first pinball machines with flippers appeared in 1947.

(368) Jeff Goldblum said The Catcher in the Rye was his favourite novel.

(369) A 2003 survey in Britain voted The Catcher in the Rye the 15th best novel in history.

(370) Salinger is believed to have written Catcher on a Hermes typewriter.

(371) The words depressed or depressing are mentioned fifty times in Catcher.

(372) Phoebe's favourite film is Alfred Hitchcock's version of The 39 Steps. This was JD Salinger's favourite film too. He would always run the film on his projector if he had guests.

(373) A British first edition of Catcher with the Fritz Wegner cover can go for over £500 in auctions. The value will be increased if the book is in good condition.

(374) Dave Eggers' A Heartbreaking Work of Staggering Genius is another novel that seems to be partly inspired by The Catcher in the Rye.

(375) When he is with Bernice, Marty, and Laverne, Holden

opines that the women would be better off going to the Stork Club if they want to see any famous people. Salinger and
Oona O'Neil used to go to the Stork Club when they were a couple.

(376) A parent group in New Jersey cited 'premarital sex, homosexuality, and perversion' for why they wanted Catcher banned in 1951.

(377) The Catcher in the Rye and John Steinbeck's Of Mice and Men were the books that received the most complaints in America in 1951.

(378) In 1963, parents of children at a school in Ohio tried to get The Catcher in the Rye banned because they argued it was prejudiced against white people. This would surely rank as one of the most bizarre and perplexing complaints against the book.

(379) The Catcher in the Rye might have arrived earlier were it not for the war. Were it not for the war though it might have been a very different book. As we have noted, some scholars believe that Catcher is a disguised war novel.

(380) Salinger was a famously slow writer. He would spend days rewriting and editing passages. It was probably unrealistic to expect him to churn out more novels after The Catcher in the Rye.

(381) Charles Bukowski said he was a big fan of The Catcher in the Rye.

(382) The name 'Sally' is used 54 times in the novel. This is four more times than 'Jane' is used.

(383) The Catcher in the Rye is called Zabhegyező in

Hungary. This translates to 'oatmeal' in English!

(384) The movie Digby Goes Down owes something to The Catcher in the Rye.

(385) The Catcher in the Rye is called Forbandede Ungdom in Denmark. This translates as Damned Youth.

(386) Wendy Torrance is seen reading The Catcher in the Rye in Kubrick's film version of The Shining.

(387) The 2000 film Finding Forrester, which had Sean Connery as a reclusive author who wrote a famous book decades ago, is clearly based on Salinger and Catcher.

(388) You could argue that Holden's dislike of Ossenburger reflects a flaw in Holden's character. Holden doesn't really know Ossenburger. He is merely judging him on one speech. Holden is perhaps too quick to see the worst in everyone he meets.

(389) Before Catcher, it was common to censor swear words in novels by altering the. F***, for example, might become fug. Catcher didn't do this.

(390) The South Park episode The Tale of Scrotie McBoogerballs is inspired by Catcher's (alleged) controversial reputation as a book that has inspired killers and been banned.

(391) Parents groups complained about underage drinking in Catcher when it came out. Despite being sixteen, Holden is always trying to get alcohol in a bar.

(392) Holden uses the word 'hell' about 63 times in the novel.

(393) Holden gives the nuns the exact same amount of money that he had to give Maurice.

(394) In WP Kinsella's 1982 novel Shoeless Joe, the main character kidnaps JD Salinger.

(395) The word 'damn' is used about 40 times in the book.

(396) The language in Catcher seems very tame today. It's hard to believe anyone was ever offended by liberal use of words like 'goddamn' and 'hell'.

(397) When Holden uses the word 'plug', this is slang for 'shoot'.

(398) On average, 680 copies of The Catcher in the Rye are still sold every day.

(399) Salinger's favourite book was a 1952 novel called The Landsmen by Peter Martin.

(400) When Catcher was chosen as the book of the month selection, they asked Salinger to change the title. Salinger wrote to them and said that Holden wouldn't like it if he changed the title.

(401) HowStuffWorks calculated that The Catcher in the Rye is the seventh biggest selling book of all time.

(402) 'Chewed the rag' means to make small talk.

(403) The Mitchell carnival horse cover remains the piece of art most associated with Catcher.

(404) Holden seems to like plays more than films. He is still a tough audience though and critical of these too.

(405) A 'matinee' is an afternoon performance.

(406) Holden likes the word 'swanky'. This means posh.

(407) Time Magazine included Catcher on their list of the 100 Best English Language novels since 1923.

(408) 'Tossed his cookies' means to vomit.

(409) Holden says that apart from D.B his favourite author is Ring Lardner.

(410) Ed Banky is the basketball coach at Pencey. Ed Banky is the name of a character in the Kevin Smith film Chasing Amy.

(411) By 1962, Catcher had sold more than two million copies.

(412) A big theme in Catcher seems to be how families find it difficult to communicate with one another. Holden steadfastly avoids his parents in the book.

(413) In 1962, college professors in California had Catcher at number one on the list of books they wanted their students to study.

(414) In a letter written to a teacher named Donald Fiene in 1960, Salinger said the controversy and censorship surrounding Catcher was something that distressed him but that he had decided to ignore it because it was out of his control.

(415) When Salinger died in 2010, online book retailers ran out of copies of The Catcher in the Rye - such was the demand.

(416) Holden likes the fact that Jane keeps her checker kings at the back of the board because she is not playing the game in a win at all costs way. She is simply enjoying the game in her own eccentric way. Holden would like this to be everyone's approach to life.

(417) The symbolism of horses in Catcher is apt. Holden has to jump the 'fences' into adulthood.

(418) The Catcher in the Rye returned to the New York Times bestseller list in 1961.

(419) The Catcher in the Rye is dedicated to Salinger's mother.

(420) Salinger was a fan of jazz and collected records. One can see this influence in Catcher.

(421) Holden thinks that Pencey is very phony to use horses to advertise the school. There are no horses at Pencey but the school gives the impression that all the students are constantly having horse-riding lessons.

(422) Salinger got a reputation for being litigious because he tried to block biographies and publication of his letters and old stories. He was simply trying to protect his work and his privacy.

(423) Salinger did not like hanging around with other writers in real life.

(424) The Catcher in the Rye is set in the winter. The chilly New York atmosphere is very apt.

(425) Salinger is said to have been interested in astrology.

(426) The 90 page novella version of Catcher was nearly

submitted for publication until Salinger changed his mind and decided to expand the book.

(427) Catcher fan art and foreign covers sometimes have Holden with shaggy hair. However, in the novel Holden tells us that he has a crew cut.

(428) Holden seems to have a dislike of corny war films.

(429) Sally tells Holden if they run away together they will probably run out of money and starve. She is being rational and realistic. This illustrates that Holden has lost his ability to make sensible and rational decisions.

(430) Holden's brother D.B served in the war and seems to have little time for the army. Salinger however kept in touch with army colleagues his whole life and would drive around Cornish in an army jeep.

(431) The fact that Salinger had published anything after 1951 simply made Catcher more of a cult book.

(432) Salinger went to a lot of bars and jazz clubs in his youth. One can see this influence in Holden's New York adventure.

(433) Although Holden says he hates Hollywood, he is always talking about movies or acting out scenes from them.

(434) At the end of Catcher, Holden realises that the cherished qualities of Allie can live on in his sister Phoebe.

(435) Some educators think that Catcher isn't relevant anymore and should be taken off curriculums.

(436) Most of Salinger's stories were about young people or

children.

(437) Salinger moved into a New York apartment after Catcher came out and painted the walls black.

(438) Salinger was in the British Isles when Catcher came out in America. He went to London, the Yorkshire Moors, Stratford Upon Avon, and Scotland.

(439) Later in the novel, Holden doesn't feel like going in the museum. He has begun to realise that you can't keep life frozen.

(440) Salinger was considered eccentric for snubbing his fame but one could argue that it's the people who chase fame who are MORE eccentric.

(441) The BBC's Big Read documentary dramatised a few narrated Catcher scenes in 2003. They were threatened with legal action but nothing came of this in the end.

(442) The Bantam paperback edition was priced at 75 cents when it appeared in 1964.

(443) The Catcher in the Rye was once removed from the list of approved books in Kershaw County, South Carolina, after the local sheriff deemed part of the novel obscene.

(444) The highest Catcher reached on the New York Times bestseller list was fourth.

(445) Holden seems to be a big fan of the book Out of Africa.

(446) Rock and roll was still about three years away when Holden Caulfield left Pencey.

(447) The word 'fart' is used once in the novel.

(448) One of the reasons why parents and censorship groups seemed to hate Catcher was that it portrayed mainstream society as pretentious and fake.

(449) Ron Rosenbaum argued in Slate that it is a common mistake to see Holden as a proxy for Salinger. 'Holden is a fictional character in a novel by JD Salinger. And JD Salinger was a gifted 30-ish writer whose accomplishment in the novel was precisely the ability to distinguish and distance himself from Holden's over-the-top, hysterically polarized division of the world into pure and impure people. To observe it with beautiful verisimilitude, to sympathize with its ardent romanticism to an extent, but not to endorse its hysteria as his own. It's a mistake that any freshman English major should be able to avoid: confusing the author of a work with the fiction—and characters—he creates. Not that there's never any relation, but one should be able to read a work, to allow it to speak for itself in complex ways, to recognize it may contain conflicting points of view, without having to mind-read its dead author or map his life into his work in a simplistic way. Or reduce the work to a single point of view. The best novels resist reduction.'

(450) It is amazing how many people advised Salinger to change the title of the book. He was wise to ignore them all as The Catcher in the Rye is now an iconic book title.

(451) Holden's surname ends in the same way that David Copperfield's surname does. This doesn't feel like a coincidence.

(452) The word 'crazy' appears 77 times in Catcher.

(453) The word 'happy' appears seven times in the book.

(454) Holden hates phonies and phony conversations yet he engages in phony conversation himself on the train.

(455) Holden professes to hate games and sport and yet he mentions playing golf several times and likes tennis.

(456) One could argue that Holden is an unreliable narrator. He is telling his tale from a very jaundiced one-sided view. We don't know what he might have left out.

(457) The red hunting hat is a symbol of Holden's confusion. He thinks he can hide underneath it but in reality it would only make him stand out.

(458) After Salinger died, Catcher became a bestseller in America again. Not bad for such an old book.

(459) Holden finds the visit to Mr Spencer uncomfortable because Spencer reminds Holden of sickness and death.

(460) Salinger performs a great feat in making us care about Holden. Few readers have any experience of boarding school or living near Central Park. However, the confusion and angst of Holden is universal.

(461) The snowball (that Holden can't bring himself to release) represents contained emotions.

(462) Holden seems wary of affection and anyone who is tactile. This suggests his parents were cold and distant.

(463) In the film and stage play Six Degrees of Separation, the main character offers a lengthy interpretation of The Catcher in the Rye.

(464) A brief memo that Salinger once penned for his cleaner fetched $50,000 at an auction.

(465) Holden namechecks the book The Return of the Native by Thomas Hardy.

(466) Ron Rosenbaum argued in Slate that Phoebe and Mr Antolini (specifically when he gives the speech about how Holden is heading for a fall) are as much avatars for Salinger as Holden is - even more so perhaps.

(467) Fredrik Colting tried to defend his book 60 Years Later: Coming Through the Rye on the grounds that it was merely a parody. The courts in America did not agree with this.

(468) In the court case against Fredrik Colting, the court stated that 'the publishing of 60 Years and similar widespread works could substantially harm the market for a Catcher sequel or other derivative works, whether through confusion as to which is the true sequel or companion to Catcher, or simply because of reduced novelty or press coverage.' While this was legally sound and correct it was also amusing. The idea that a 90 year-old JD Salinger was going to write The Catcher in the Rye Part 2 was of course preposterous.

(469) Salinger is commonly alleged to have used his memories of Valley Forge when describing the look of Pencey.

(470) The Mitchell carnival horse cover 'impalement' could be read to be symbolic of the fact that childhood must end.

(471) Holden is true to his promise at the start of the book and doesn't reveal much about his childhood in the pages that follow.

(472) Despite his barbs, Holden admits that Pencey is a

school that has good academic success. They don't tolerate failing grades.

(473) Joyce Maynard, who left Yale and went live with Salinger in Cornish when she was 18 in 1972, said that she had never read The Catcher in the Rye when Salinger started writing to her.

(474) Salinger gives Holden a faulty memory at times where our narrator says he can't quite remember something. This is designed to make Holden more trustworthy when it comes to things he does remember.

(475) The Guardian obituary for Salinger was written by an academic who had been dead for seven years. Newspaper obits are often written when celebrities are still alive so they are ready to be published at any time.

(476) According to the New York Times obituary, Salinger asked his agent to burn any fan mail after Catcher came out. This seems a dubious 'fact' though because there are instances of Salinger responding to letters. Some fan mail must have got through to him.

(477) The word 'stupid' is used 46 times in Catcher.

(478) Jane's strategy in checkers suggests she is adverse to risk. Something in life has made her nervous.

(479) In her memoir Dream Catcher, Salinger's daughter Margaret said that JD Salinger (who was into alternative health remedies) drank his own urine. This is known as urine therapy, urophagia, or urotherapy. Although some people do this for health reasons there is said to be no scientific evidence that it is beneficial.

(480) In the case involving Fredrik Colting and 60 Years

Later: Coming Through the Rye, the court 'believed that Colting took well more from Catcher, in both substance and style, than is necessary for the alleged transformative purpose of criticizing Salinger and his attitudes and behavior. However, for the non-parodic purpose of commenting upon Salinger, rather than his work, it was unnecessary for Colting to use the same protagonist with repeated and extensive detail and allusion to the original work.'

(481) Catcher is a pretty short novel by most standards. 187 pages in the Penguin paperback version.

(482) The driver refuses to allow Holden on the bus with a snowball because he doesn't believe Holden won't throw it. Holden is irritated by this and yet he shares something in common with the bus driver. They both see only the worst in people and don't give them the benefit of the doubt.

(483) The connection between John Hinckley Jr is what you could call somewhat unfair or overblown. A copy of The Catcher in the Rye was found in his hotel room but there were a dozen or so other books too. No one sought to blame any of these books for his actions.

(484) When Holden asks Stradlater if Jane still keeps her checker kings at the back of the board the subtext is clearly how far Stradlater got with her sexually. Holden wants to still think of Jane as a virginal shy girl with her checker kings stationary.

(485) There is another Dickens link in Catcher because Freddie Bartholomew, who Holden apparently resembles, was in a film version of David Copperfield.

(486) Holden is depressed by the elderly 'bellboy' at the Edmont Hotel. This man reinforces Holden's view that life

is unfair.

(487) Anne L. Goodman gave Catcher a sniffy review when it was published. 'Holden Caulfield, the main character who tells his own story, is an extraordinary portrait, but there is too much of him. In the course of 277 pages, the reader wearies of [his] explicitness, repetition and adolescence, exactly as one would weary of Holden himself. And this reader at least suffered from an irritated feeling that Holden was not quite so sensitive and perceptive as he, and his creator, thought he was. In any case he is so completely self-centered that the other characters who wander through the book—with the notable exception of his sister Phoebe—have nothing like his authenticity. In a writer of Salinger's undeniable talent, one expects something more.'

(488) The Perks of Being a Wallflower clearly takes some inspiration from Catcher.

(489) Ohio, Alabama, Florida, North Dakota, California, Mississippi, Illinois, and New Hampshire all saw parent protests against Catcher when it was published.

(490) A brass ring is a small grabbable ring that a dispenser presents to a carousel rider during the course of a ride. You get a prize if you grab the 'gold' ring.

(491) At the end of the novel, Holden accepts that children have to grab the 'gold ring' in the end. The gold ring in this case is adulthood.

(492) Isolation is a big theme in the novel. Despite being in a boarding school and then a big city, Holden feels alone.

(493) JD Salinger did not write The Catcher in the Rye for a teenage audience. He saw it as an adult book.

(494) 'Hound's-tooth' is a pattern of jagged checks.

(495) Holden's refusal to actually meet up with Jane reduces her to a fantasy or memory rather than a real person. Holden, in his confused state, is choosing fantasy over reality - a path which is not sustainable forever.

(496) Charles Bukowski said of Salinger - "Catcher in the Rye is really great. You see, it's about young people going through their thing, but it's so well done...maybe when he got past the young people thing, that was all there was...it would be sad if it was so."

(497) Salinger said the 1950 short story For Esmé with Love and Squalor gave him the confidence to complete The Catcher in the Rye.

(498) When it was first published, there were protests against Catcher in Canada from parent and religious groups.

(499) The Book Review's James Stern complained that The Catcher in the Rye was too long when it came out. Stern thought that Salinger was a short story writer and should stick to that.

(500) Joyce Maynard said that when she lived with Salinger he sometimes used to have frozen peas for his breakfast.

(501) When Salinger was at Valley Forge, pupils had red flashes in their caps as punishment for bad language. Those in and around the school were supposed to snub the pupils with red in their hats to teach them a lesson. It is possible that this memory gave Salinger the inspiration for Holden's red hat.

(502) Norman Mailer once called JD Salinger "the greatest mind to ever stay in prep school."

(503) Jay McInerney once said - "Reading Catcher in the Rye made me want to live in New York City and go to the bars where Holden went and walk in his fictional steps through Central Park. For all of its satire, Catcher in the Rye is a very romantic portrait of New York."

(504) A copy of The Catcher in the Rye was found on Lee Harvey Oswald's book case.

(505) Gladstone is a type of luggage.

(506) Clavichord is a type of keyboard instrument. Holden misuses this word for comic effect.

(507) Although he didn't want a Catcher film, Salinger was eager for his story The Laughing Man to become a movie. No one ever showed sufficient interest in adapting it though.

(508) Holden's red hunting hat is mentioned 39 times in the novel.

(509) The New York Public Library exhibited some items that belonged to Salinger in 2019. The exhibition included Salinger's original typescript of Catcher with hand-written revisions.

(510) Catcher didn't win a Pulitzer Prize. In 1952 the award went to The Caine Mutiny by Herman Wouk.

(511) It is estimated that around 250,000 copies of The Catcher in the Rye are sold each year.

(512) 'Swell' means good.

(513) Pedagogical means in relation to the work of a teacher.

(514) Tattersall is a cloth pattern.

(515) Salinger briefly considered in the 1950s putting the option of his family selling the Catcher film rights in his will in case anything happened to him. This would have been a very good insurance policy. Although he never did it in the end, the appeal of this to Salinger was that he wouldn't be around to see the film!

(516) In their 1951 review of Catcher, Booklist warned readers that the novel contained 'coarse language.'

(517) Salinger was calculated to have had a fortune of around $20 million when he passed away.

(518) 'Falsies' are breast enhancers.

(519) The Catcher in the Rye expresses a fear that human values have been eroded by the pursuit of money and power.

(520) A wooden press is a case for a tennis racket.

(521) Halitosis means to have bad breath.

(522) It is said that Salinger never followed the dress code at Valley Forge and always had a rumpled uniform.

(523) Peter Lorre was a famous actor. He was in films like Casablanca.

(524) 'Backasswards' means back to front or out of order.

(525) 'Faggy' means weary or tired.

(526) Like his hero Holden Caulfield, Salinger's top subject at school was English.

(527) Salinger's son Matt said that the reason his father hated the idea of a Catcher film is that readers would then always picture Holden in the book as the actor who played him in the movie. JD Salinger wanted the reader to have to imagine Holden themselves.

(528) There seem to be no recordings of Salinger's speaking voice.

(529) Those who knew Salinger or viewed him in court say he had a very deep and rich voice.

(530) 'Necked' means kissed or to kiss.

(531) Salinger was fond of poetry and wrote poems during the war.

(532) Holden losing the school fencing equipment on the subway is Salinger's early way of telling us that Holden lacks maturity and responsibility.

(533) The actor Ethan Hawke once said in an interview - "When you're depressed, it's really easy to see everything that is fake about other people and life, and I just started seeing all that. How phony celebrity was, how phony everything is. You channel your inner Holden Caulfield, you know?"

(534) Within the first 2 months of publication, Catcher was reprinted 8 times.

(535) Salinger has been accused of having a very constrictive range of characters when it comes to social class. It is true that many of his characters were arty or financially comfortable Manhattan types.

(536) You can buy a leather bound edition of Catcher for about $80.

(537) The 1984 novel Bright Lights, Big City by Jay McInerney clearly owes something to Catcher.

(538) Before the war, Salinger briefly worked as an entertainer on a Swedish cruise liner.

(539) The Catcher in the Rye is called El vigilant en el camp de sègol in Catalan. In English this translates as The watchman in the rye field.

(540) Although published in the early 1950s, Catcher is a very 1940s novel. There is, for example, no mention of television.

(541) Salinger believed that nothing should get in the way between the reader and the words. This is why he disliked fancy book covers or a foreward.

(542) 'Cockeyed' means tilted to one side.

(543) At college, Salinger took a writing course by Whit Burnett.

(544) Whit Burnett is often credited with encouraging Salinger to write a longer more autobiographical book rather than simply focus on short stories. Burnett could then plausibly take some credit for planting the seed of what became Catcher.

(545) Holden grows weary of Sally because she believes people should follow the 'rules' in life.

(546) Those who knew Salinger at school say he was rather bored by formal education and couldn't seem to apply himself. Holden shares the same quality.

(547) Holden's personality changes when he puts on his red hunting hat. It is like he uses the hat to hide in another character.

(548) As things currently stand, The Catcher in the Rye will enter public domain in 2046.

(549) It is sort of absurd that people still write articles suggesting that The Catcher in the Rye has a psychotic fan base. As Matt Salinger pointed out, two crazy people out of 70 million read Catcher and did something bad. That's not exactly a high amount!

(550) It is said that Salinger ate a lot of raw foods because he believed the cooking process destroyed nutrients.

(551) Salinger used double-spaces when he typed Catcher.

(552) Salinger was a follower of homeopathy.

(553) Holden is vaguely catty about Hemingway's A Farewell to Arms. Salinger was friends with Hemingway in real life.

(554) In 1961, Catcher was dropped from school curriculums in San Jose after protests.

(555) After the success of Catcher, Salinger was offered some academic 'guest' teaching positions at schools and colleges. He declined all of these.

(556) Catcher had sold 15 million copies by 1996.

(557) Holden's red hunting hat cost him one dollar.

(558) One could argue that the memoir Girl, Interrupted by Susanna Kaysen, though a true story, owes something to the spirit of Catcher.

(559) Salinger made a Time magazine list of the ten most reclusive celebrities. Greta Garbo and Howard Hughes were top of the pile.

(560) Holden's father is a corporation lawyer. The Caulfield family are financially comfortable.

(561) Catcher is mentioned in Billy Joel's song We didn't start the fire.

(562) An early edition of Catcher with the James Avati cover can sell for $100.

(563) Louis Menand said · 'Salinger is imagined to have given voice to what every adolescent, or at least, every sensitive, intelligent, middle-class adolescent, thinks, but is too inhibited to say, which is that success is a sham, and that successful people are mostly phonies.'

(564) In his biography of Salinger, Paul Alexander suggested that Salinger's vanishing act was actually a clever way to promote his old books (and thus ensure an income) without actually having to produce new work. 'By cutting himself off from the public, by cutting himself off the way he had done, he had made sure the public would remain fascinated with him. By refusing to publish any new work, by letting the public know he had new work he was not publishing, he ensured a continued fascination in

the four books that were in print. But that was not enough. To guarantee that there was no way the public could forget him, he periodically surfaced in the press by doing something that was sure to attract publicity...the way Salinger handled the publicity he said he did not want was a bit too contrived to get attention itself. Salinger became the Greta Garbo of literature, and then periodically, when it may have seemed he was about to be forgotten, he resurfaced briefly, just to remind the public that he wanted to be left alone. The whole act could have been cute or whimsical; only, it felt as if it were being put on by a master showman, a genius spin doctor, a public-relations wizard hawking a story the public couldn't get enough of.'

(565) The Catcher in the Rye is called De veghe în lanul de secară in Romanian. In English this translates as Watching in the rye field.

(566) The fact that Holden is on some deeper spiritual quest is highlighted by him not understanding simple things in life like why the result of a football match matters or why people care if their car gets a scratch.

(567) Salinger always refused to allow his work to appear in anthologies.

(568) Holden says he studied Beowulf when he was at Whooton School.

(569) The irony of protests against the bad language in Catcher is that Holden is trying to PROTECT children from the f-word.

(570) Holden seems to despise popular culture.

(571) Carl Luce appears in the 1946 Caulfield story Slight Rebellion off Madison.

(572) Joanna Rakoff, who worked for Salinger's agents in the 1990s, said she was told that if she ever spoke to Salinger she was never to mention The Catcher the Rye.

(573) A Lithuanian cover for The Catcher in the Rye is one of the most bizarre. It depicts red silhouettes of Holden and a girl floating over an abstract New York like Peter Pan.

(574) Jay McInerney said of Catcher - "Catcher in the Rye injected a fresh idiom into American literature. This happened several times in our literary history. Mark Twain in Huckleberry Finn and Ernest Hemingway in The Sun Also Rises did the same – they brought the contemporary spoken language into literature. When Salinger invented Holden Caulfield he gave his voice such freshness and vibrancy. Salinger also almost invented the concept of teenage angst – Salinger's was the first voice of the youthquake that transformed our society in the 50s, 60s and 70s."

(575) A Swedish Catcher in the Rye book cover by Albert Bonniers förlag is rather odd. It features a pin-up girl and a duck!

(576) Holden deduces over the course of Catcher that he is too quick to judge people. You can't make an assessment of people you've only just met - like Holden often does in the novel.

(577) Salinger was apparently pretty deaf after the war and so you had to shout if you were talking on the phone to him.

(578) Holden seems to associate the flannel suit (which was of course very popular at the time) with conformity and assimilation.

(579) Jefferson Singer wrote of Catcher · 'Accessible to younger readers, and filled with cynicism and humor about the rather pathetic adult world, it was irresistible for any adolescent with a hint of rebellion. At the same time, there was an adult mind guiding our relationship to Holden and we could feel its questioning presence as it let us see Holden's pretensions and fears. Salinger gave to adolescent readers a character speaking to us in our own voice that we could simultaneously identify with and step back from. We could ache with love for him, even as we somehow knew we were at that very place where we soon leave him behind. Whether Salinger himself could ever let go of Holden is a question that biographers will now be hustling to resolve once and for all, but this reclusive genius's ironic legacy can be found in how many of my generation he pushed forward into the adult world.'

(580) Although he was said to hate technology, Salinger apparently had an email account before he died.

(581) The actor Freddie Highmore once said it had been his dream as a child actor to play Holden Caulfield one day.

(582) Harvey Swados called Salinger the "Greta Garbo of American letters."

(583) The Catcher in the Rye is one of Modern Library's best 100 English language novels in the 20th century.

(584) A Russian Catcher in the Rye book cover has Holden praying in a field of rye. It's not one of the best.

(585) Catcher is regarded by many to be a picaresque novel. A picaresque novel is usually a first-person narrative, relating the adventures of a rogue or lowborn adventurer.

(586) Holden feels inferior to Phoebe and Allie so it makes

sense that he would wear a red hunting hat to feel more like them. Holden does not have red hair like his two younger siblings.

(587) A hardback copy of the 1994 Catcher reissue by Hamish Hamilton can sell for over £50.

(588) A number of readers have detected a homoerotic element in Catcher. Holden constantly tells us how handsome Stradlater is. Holden is also sexually confused (read by some people as code for gay) and declines to do anything with the female prostitute Sunny.

(589) In 1961, an unemployed former child actor named Bill Mahan tracked Salinger down in Cornish to ask for the rights to make a Catcher film. He approached Salinger in the street and was given a polite but firm rejection.

(590) The book critic Jonathan Yardley wrote · 'The Catcher in the Rye is now, you'll be told just about anywhere you ask, an American classic, right up there with the book that was published the following year, Ernest Hemingway's The Old Man and the Sea. They are two of the most durable and beloved books in American literature and, by any reasonable critical standard, two of the worst. Rereading The Catcher in the Rye after all those years was almost literally a painful experience: The combination of Salinger's execrable prose and Caulfield's jejune narcissism produced effects comparable to mainlining castor oil. The cheap sentimentality with which the novel is suffused reaches a climax of sorts when Holden's literary side comes to the fore. He flunks all his courses except English. 'I'm quite illiterate,' he says early in the book, 'but I read a lot,' which establishes the mixture of self-deprecation and self-congratulation that seems to appeal to so many readers. Salinger has a tin ear. His characters forever say 'ya' for 'you,' as in 'ya know,' which no American except perhaps a

slapstick comedian ever has said. Americans say 'yuh know' or 'y'know,' but never 'ya know.'

(591) A Burmese cover for Catcher was one of the worst. It depicts a fairly mature looking man (presumably supposed to be Holden) who appears Asian.

(592) Despite his reputation as a fad health food nut, in private letters Salinger expressed a fondness for Burger King.

(593) James Jones' From Here to Eternity sold more copies than Catcher when they both came out around the same time. Catcher's popularity was more enduring though.

(594) Salinger always tried to block his early stories from being published again because he felt he had a big ego when he was younger and he believed his ego came through in those early stories.

(595) Salinger enjoyed fencing in his youth. Fencing gets a mention at the start of Catcher.

(596) It is rather ironic that at one time Catcher was simultaneously the most studied and the most banned book in America.

(597) Salinger ended World War 2 in a hospital suffering from combat stress.

(598) 'Ostracize' means to exclude.

(599) Holden is touched by the fact that Jane always left her kings in checkers at the back of the board. Holden admires the fact that Jane refused to adhere to the conventions of the game.

(600) Danish filmmaker Henning Carlsen wrote to Salinger in 1967 in an attempt to gain permission to make A Catcher in the Rye film but had no more luck than anyone else in this matter. Salinger wrote back to Carlsen and said that he had no particular 'beef' with the film industry but simply didn't want to sell the film rights.

(601) 'Yap' means mouth (as in keep your yap shut).

(602) 578,141 paperback copies of The Catcher in the Rye were sold in 2010.

(603) Literary critic Clifton Fadiman wrote of Catcher · "That rare miracle of fiction has again come to pass: a human being has been created out of ink, paper, and the imagination."

(604) Alberto Fuguet's 1991 novel Mala onda has many references to The Catcher in the Rye.

(605) The Catcher in the Rye has been branded communist propaganda by some of those seeking to censor it · although there is little evidence that JD Salinger was a communist.

(606) Jitterbugging is a fast athletic type of dancing.

(607) Salinger said he was a 'dash man not a miler'. This meant he felt much more comfortable writing sort stories. It was difficult for him to write something as long as Catcher and he never did so again.

(608) When Holden imagines a future in which he is working in an office and riding Madison Avenue buses he is dismayed by this conventional picture of what lies ahead. He doesn't want to be like everyone else of his own age and class.

(609) The actress Winona Ryder said - "It's weird because when you first read that book, it's so personal and you feel like you're the only one who feels that way, and then you realize that everyone has had that experience with it. But Holden Caulfield was like my best friend when I was a teenager. Salinger is someone whose work I just love so much, and I totally respect how protective he has been about his privacy."

(610) A stenographer is a person who has an expertise in writing with shorthand methods.

(611) Holden says that the expensive schools have the most crooks. This represents the contempt Holden has for the system. Those who are rich or upper class are no different from criminals in Holden's mind.

(612) Lord Randal My Son is a 17th century Anglo-Scottish border ballad.

(613) A 'stink' is slang for creating a fuss or controversy.

(614) Holden doesn't usually wear his hunting hat if he's going to be around people. The hat represents the tension within Holden over the need for both companionship and isolation.

(615) 'Oodles' means a lot.

(616) Finlo Rohrer, writing for the BBC, said Catcher is the defining work on what it is like to be a teenager.

(617) The Ziegfeld Follies was a series of theatrical revue productions on Broadway.

(618) Holden finds New York to be a lonely place when he leaves Pencey. Big cities, despite being full of people and

noise, can often be alienating and lonely places.

(619) A 'half gainer' is an elaborate dive or backflip.

(620) Holden doesn't like the idea of exclusive boarding schools because he doesn't want to belong to anything exclusive or snooty. You could say that Salinger felt the same. Salinger didn't want to belong to anything at all.

(621) Two episodes of The Twilight Zone have a theme of escape that is very similar to The Catcher in the Rye. Both were made in 1959. Walking Distance is about a stressed executive who wants to escape the rat race and recapture his small town youth. A Stop at Willoughby is also about a weary executive who dreams of turning back time and living in a quiet bucolic town.

(622) The Salvation Army is a Christian church and charitable organisation. It was founded in England in 1865.

(623) It is said that Salinger once got very furious when a proofreader added a single comma to one of his short stories.

(624) Romeo and Juliet is one of the most famous plays written by William Shakespeare. Holden seems to have a particular fondness for the character Mercutio.

(625) Flys Up is a softball playground game.

(626) An Azerbaijani cover for The Catcher in the Rye has a big picture of Salinger on the cover. Salinger would have absolutely hated that.

(627) In 1982, school libraries in Morris, Manitoba banned Catcher because it violated their rules on books not featuring 'excess vulgar language, sexual scenes, things

concerning moral issues, excessive violence, and anything dealing with the occult.'

(628) The novel A Complicated Kindness by Miriam Toews owes something to Catcher.

(629) Shadow punching means to throw punches at an imaginary opponent (in the way that boxers shadow box in the gym).

(630) Sally wants to go skating so she can wear her skating skirt. This suggests vanity - something that Holden probably doesn't approve of.

(631) Judas is a reference to the disciple who betrayed Jesus.

(632) In chapter 13, Holden mentions Monsieur Blanchard. This could be a reference to a 1928 book called Warped in the Making: Crimes of Love and Hate.

(633) Holden's fascination with the Egyptian mummies signifies a preoccupation with death.

(634) 'Furlough' is a temporary layoff or break.

(635) A polo coat is a loose coat often made of camel hair.

(636) Bridge is a popular card game.

(637) There were over seven million television sets in American homes by the time Catcher was published.

(638) Sally is depicted as a very conventional woman of her time in that she doesn't seem to question a future that is already mapped out for her. Holden dislikes this type of conventional attitude.

(639) When Catcher was in the process of publication, Salinger sent his publishers a note with his thoughts of what shade of colour should be used on the cover. Salinger was apparently of the mind that the book should have a brown cover.

(640) When Catcher came out, Atlantic Monthly called Holden an 'urban, transplanted Huck Finn.'

(641) A 2015 a movie called Coming Through the Rye was based on James Steven Sadwith's attempt to track down JD Salinger when he was a teenager to gain permission to adapt Catcher as a school play.

(642) James Steven Sadwith said he put on the Catcher school play anyway even though Salinger had declined to give permission. Sadwith said Salinger was quite polite though and even offered him a lift to the station.

(643) In a quirk of fate, James Steven Sadwith said that in the late 1980s he was doing auditions for a TV miniseries and Matt Salinger was one of the actors who turned up to audition. He didn't cast him though.

(644) James Steven Sadwith offered Matt Salinger a part in his 2015 film Coming Through the Rye. Matt Salinger declined the offer though because he didn't want to be in a film about his father.

(645) Bloomingdale's is a Manhattan department store.

(646) A 'rake' in catcher is an immoral person - a cad or bounder.

(647) 'Ratty' means dirty or shabby.

(648) The cover for the 1964 Bantam edition of Catcher is Exeter crimson. That's a fancy way of saying dark red.

(649) The 1964 Bantam edition of Catcher has a gold serif font.

(650) A Portuguese cover for Catcher appears to depict Holden and Sunny together.

(651) A 'loafer' is a shoe like a moccasin with a flat heel.

(652) When Holden refers to someone as a 'prince', this means a generous good hearted person. Sometimes though the reference is sarcastic.

(653) The Holland Tunnel is a tunnel under the Hudson River.

(654) It is estimated that about 400,000 copies of Catcher were published each year in the mid 1980s.

(655) A 'glider' in Catcher is a name for a porch seat.

(656) Salinger uses a lot of digressions in Catcher.

(657) Annapolis is the capital of Maryland.

(658) Salinger and E. Michael Mitchell fell out in the end. Mitchell even sold the letters he received from Salinger after Salinger's death. It is alleged that they fell out because Salinger snubbed Mitchell's request to autograph a copy of The Catcher in the Rye for him.

(659) Catcher had sold about nine million copies by 1975.

(660) In 1990, some new editions of Catcher and other works were due to be prepared so Salinger sent a note to

the publishers with his thoughts on what the covers should look like. 'All four book titles to be printed in jet-black ink. In plain simple type, much like 36 Point Caslon 540 ATF. I would prefer, of course, that the title and author's name be placed lower, more nearly centered on the cover than outlined in the attached sketch ... Bantam thought my original mid-cover placement of the title for Franny and Zooey not suitable for ordinary sales-rack display. (So I added thin green parallel bars across lower third of the corner, to compensate for any imbalance, top-heaviness, or placing the title too high at the top. I think my vivid diagonal bars should carry things off nicely enough.)'

(661) Holden is uplifted by his meeting with the nuns because they show him that not all adults have to become phonies.

(662) Salinger uses Italics in Catcher to emphasise certain words.

(663) Tobias Wolff said of Catcher - '[Holden]'s a very, very funny fellow. And he's very acute in spotting phonies. The problem with Holden is that, to him, everyone, after a while, seems phony. As funny the book as it is, and reading through it again recently, I found it devastatingly sad. His younger brother who he has idolized for his innocence -the way he now does his sister Phoebe – has died. And he ruminates on the – on going to his grave and being caught in a downpour and thinking of leaving his brother there underground in this terrible day. And later, he himself is walking along the street in New York. And it should be festive. It's around Christmastime. The shoppers are out. And he is broken into a sweat. Every time he steps off the curb, he thinks I'm going to go down and down forever. No one will ever see me again. This kind of calls up that image of his brother in his grave. And he starts praying to his brother – Allie, don't let me disappear. Don't let me

disappear. There's such terror there. The humor that has sustained so much of this novel begins to unravel at the end and you're left with this naked soul in pain and in conflict.'

(664) Valley Forge had a cannon on top of a hill like Pencey Prep.

(665) TheGreatestBooks.Org ranked Catcher the 6th greatest novel of all time.

(666) 'Sterling' means good or excellent.

(667) The novel The Miseducation of Cameron Post by Emily M. Danforth owes something to The Catcher in the Rye.

(668) Simon Prosser, of Hamish Hamilton, said - "There are strict rules about JD Salinger's covers. The only copy allowed on the books, back or front, is the author name and the title. Nothing else at all: no quotes, no cover blurb, no biography. We're not really sure why this is, but it gives you definite guidelines. Last year we decided it was probably time to re-design the covers, and we wanted a unique typeface that stood out. We commissioned Seb Lester, the highly regarded type designer, to hand-draw a font; that font, on the cover of these re-issues, is a one-off and is known in-house here at Hamish Hamilton as the 'Salinger.'"

(669) in 1974, Salinger broke a long silence to express his irritation at the unauthorised underground release of a compilation titled The Complete Uncollected Short Stories of JD Salinger, Vols. 1 and 2. ""Some stories, my property, have been stolen," said Salinger. "Someone's appropriated them. It's an illicit act. It's unfair. Suppose you had a coat you liked and somebody went into your closet and stole it. That's how I feel. I pay for this kind of attitude. I'm known

as a strange, aloof kind of man. But all I'm doing is trying to protect myself and my work. I just want all this to stop. It's intrusive. I've survived a lot of things and I'll probably survive this."

(670) All the supporting characters in Catcher are designed to shed light on Holden's personality.

(671) A 'hoodlum' is a gangster or thuggish criminal type of person.

(672) There is a famous conspiracy theory that Salinger and Thomas Pynchon are the same person.

(673) Salinger uses the device of unfinished sentences in Catcher. This illustrates the doubt and confusion of the main character.

(674) The famous Mitchell carnival horse cover has a hand-lettered font.

(675) Catcher is an example of a bildungsroman novel. This means a novel dealing with one person's formative years or spiritual education.

(676) The Catcher in the Rye is a very episodic novel. One can see how a number of short stories formed the basis for the book.

(677) 'Pansy' is slang for an effeminate or weak man.

(678) A lagoon is a pond like body of water.

(679) Salinger's stories are very suspicious and wary of the post-war prosperity in America. Salinger's believes that a material and consumer driven society will erode basic human values.

(680) Of his reluctance to send out advance copies or do any publicity, Salinger explained himself by saying to his publishers - "I can't explain what I mean. And even if I could, I'm not sure I'd feel like it."

(681) A Persian cover of Catcher has a crow on the cover.

(682) The novel Prep by Curtis Sittenfeld clearly has some Catcher influences.

(683) 'Muckle-mouthed' means to distort one's mouth when speaking.

(684) When Salinger wrote Catcher in Westport he is believed to have lived on Old Road, off the Post Road. His exact address there is not known.

(685) In a private letter published after his death, Salinger described fellow writers as 'hopeless megalomaniacs.'

(686) Woody Allen said of Catcher - "It was amusing, it was in my vernacular, and the atmosphere held great emotional resonance for me. I reread it on a few occasions and I always get a kick out of it."

(687) Ivy League is a group of American colleges and universities with a reputation for excellence and being of a higher social standing.

(688) 'Plastered' means to get drunk.

(689) The New Yorker, declining to publish extracts from Catcher, complained to Salinger that they didn't feel that the story allowed the reader to get to know Holden Caulfield well enough. That feels like a very strange complaint given the copious introspection and endless first

person thoughts of Holden.

(690) The famous plain red cover of older Catcher editions uses the Times New Roman font.

(691) A Turkish cover for Catcher depicts a young man in glasses lying in the street as people mill around him. It is rather baffling.

(692) Catcher struck a chord in young people because Holden is against the status quo.

(693) Tobias Wolff said of Catcher · 'When I first read it, I felt as if [Holden was] a confederate of mine, you know, a teammate in this skepticism about this worthiness of adult life, and now I look at him, in a way, like his old teacher, Mr. Antolini, who pats his head while he's asleep. Then Holden wakes up from that and imagines that the man has made a pass at him he can't even accept that, that avuncular affection that the man is overcome by. And I have that avuncular affection for Holden and I have a degree of sorrow, really, that I couldn't possibly have felt at that time.'

(694) Salinger had a habit of checking into a hotel room to finish writing a story.

(695) Salinger feels very much like a time capsule relic of the 1940s. It is hard to imagine he would have ever written a novel set in the 1980s or 1990s · even though he was still alive and (apparently) still writing in those decades.

(696) In a 1979 letter to E. Michael Mitchell, JD Salinger said he no longer enjoyed visiting New York.

(697) The Rockettes are a dance company at Radio City Music Hall.

(698) The Catcher in the Rye could be described as a realist novel in that it uses slang and real locations.

(699) A Slovenian cover for Catcher by Mladinska knjiga has Holden with a vest on the cover and a tattoo on his shoulder. Salinger, for some reason, is billed as 'Jerome D Salinger' on the cover.

(700) Eustacia Vye is a character in Thomas Hardy's book The Return of the Native.

(701) Holden pretending to tapdance and calling himself the governor's son while in the bathroom with Stradlater is an allusion to the Broadway musical The Governor's Son.

(702) A Lithuanian cover for Catcher by Vaga is one of the strangest and worst. It features Holden on the cover with blond spiky hair and a leather jacket.

(703) Of Human Bondage is a 1915 novel by W. Somerset Maugham.

(704) 'Roller-skate skinny' obviously means fit and active. Someone who is slender.

(705) West Point is a famous American Military Academy. Dwight Eisenhower, George Patton, Buzz Aldrin, and Douglas MacArthur are among the many famous people to have gone to this school.

(706) Someone with a 'Holy Joe voice' is pompous and superior in tone.

(707) Raymond Goldfarb is a student Holden knew at Elkton Hills. They got drunk together in the chapel.

(708) A Polish cover for Catcher had Salinger's name bigger than the title of the novel. Salinger would have really hated that if he ever saw it.

(709) Holden's fantasy of living in a cabin in the woods could be an allusion to Henry David Thoreau's Walden; or, Life in the Woods.

(710) 'Oiled up' means drunk.

(711) The Baker's Wife is a 1938 French film directed by Marcel Pagnol.

(712) James Stern's review of Catcher for The New York Times was really annoying (or crumby if you prefer) because Stern tried to write it in the style of how Holden narrates. The New York times maybe realised this review was annoying because they soon published another review.

(713) Holden wonders where the ducks in Central Park go in the winter when the lake is frozen over. In 2001, the park commissioner, in answer to Holden's question, said, "Usually the ducks go to the middle of the lake, which is the least likely to freeze. If that freezes over they have been seen in the Hudson and East Rivers. In fact ducks travel much less than they used to, because it is really much easier for them than it was in 1951." Duck experts have suggested that the ducks would simply find a warmer place in the park if the water was frozen over with ice.

(714) 't.b.' is tuberculosis. Tuberculosis is an infection with a germ (bacterium) called Mycobacterium tuberculosis. It usually attacks the lungs.

(715) Storm shoes are boots for all types of weather.

(716) Rupert Brooke was an English poet known for his war

sonnets.

(717) Robert Tichener and Paul Campbell are the two boys that Holden recalls throwing a football around with at Pencey until it got dark. This is a rare moment where Holden has a happy memory of the school. It is ruined though by the biology teacher Mr Zambesi telling them to go back to their dorm and get ready for dinner.

(718) JD Salinger hated the fame The Catcher in the Rye gave him so much that he couldn't wait for the sales to subside.

(719) During World War 2, Salinger carried a typewriter around in his jeep.

(720) Salinger was said to have a very sarcastic sense of humour. You can obviously see evidence of this in Holden Caulfield.

(721) An irony not lost on biographers is that Salinger's refusal to be a public figure or publish much enabled him to maintain his cult status as a writer. If he had constantly appeared on television and churned out novels then Salinger would have had no mystique.

(722) Raimu was the stage name of French actor Jules Auguste Muraire.

(723) An Indonesian cover for Catcher simply had a huge eyeball with a flame inside it.

(724) Slaughter on Tenth Avenue is a ballet with music by Richard Rodgers.

(725) Dick Slagle was Holden's former roommate at Elkton Hills. The fact that Slagle had cheap suitcases always

irritated Holden.

(726) Joyce Maynard said that living with Salinger in the 1970s was like going back in time. He still listened to Glen Miller records and had no interest in modern music.

(727) The communist party in the Soviet Union approved The Catcher in the Rye because they believed it depicted American capitalism as rotten and alienating.

(728) Song of India is a popular song adapted from Rimsky-Korsakov's 1896 opera Sadko.

(729) Lastex is a type of elastic yarn that was introduced in the 1930s. It was used for swimwear, brassieres, girdles and corselettes.

(730) Robert Donat was an English actor. He starred in Phoebe's favourite film The 39 Steps.

(731) When Joyce Maynard corresponded with Salinger for the first time in the early 1970s, he told her that he was still constantly pestered by people trying to get the film rights to Catcher.

(732) Al Pike was a former date of Jane Gallagher. Jane felt sorry for Al because he had an 'inferiority complex'.

(733) Fredrik Colting (John David California) preposterously said of his crumby book 60 Years Later: Coming Through the Rye - "I think 60 Years Later IS a super-original novel. In many ways I believe 60 is as original and creative as Catcher. I realize I'm putting myself on the line saying this, but it's really a modern day Frankenstein."

(734) Salinger's family had a potted food and meat business

that made them quite wealthy. Salinger's father tried to get him involved in the business but he wasn't interested. Somehow, you can't really picture JD Salinger in charge of a canned food company.

(735) The musical Next to Normal references The Catcher in the Rye.

(736) Salinger despised the very idea of literary criticism.

(737) The Atlantic Monthly is an American magazine founded in 1857.

(738) Yellowstone National Park is a wilderness area mostly in Wyoming but the park spreads into parts of Montana and Idaho too.

(739) As a student, JD Salinger wrote a poem in the Valley Forge yearbook that became the lyrics to the school anthem.

(740) Allie died at the age of eleven.

(741) A 'strong box' is a fortified box or safe for storing valuable items.

(742) El Morocco was a hip nightclub frequented by the rich and famous. Years later, in the 1990s, it became a topless bar.

(743) A highball is typically served with ice in a straight glass.

(744) The Saturday Evening Post is an American magazine founded in 1821.

(745) A Czech cover for Catcher by Knižní klub simply has

a blue background with yellow dots. It's one of the rare foreign covers that you could probably imagine Salinger not taking offence at.

(746) 'Sack' means bed - as in hit the sack.

(747) Broadway is the home of New York's theatre district in Midtown Manhattan.

(748) 'Bourgeois' means middle-class or someone who is well off and displays quite expensive tastes.

(749) The Quakers are a group of Christians who use no scripture. They believe in a simple way of life. The movement began in Mid-17th century England.
England

(750) When Holden says if he could play the piano well he'd play in a 'goddam closet' this is rather like Salinger writing stories and sticking them in a drawer - which is exactly what he did for most of his life.

(751) Vogue is a fashion magazine first published in New York City in 1892.

(752) Salinger was said to write for up to sixteen hours a day when he finishing Catcher.

(753) Salinger was half Jewish. It is sometimes alleged that anti-Semitism in the American education system was something he detected in his own life and one of the possible reasons why Catcher doesn't care much for the school and college system.

(754) When Phoebe puts the hunting hat on Holden this is a symbol of the fact that she loves and accepts Holden for what he is.

(755) Holden says he has had his grey hairs since he was a little kid. This suggests he has always been different and at odds with the world.

(756) The Dicksteins are the Caulfields' neighbors. Holden pretends to be a Dickstein relative to get past the new elevator boy in the apartment building where his family lives.

(757) The yearning for escape is palpable in Catcher. It's no surprise that the author of the novel ducked out of the rat race and big city himself soon after the book was published.

(758) Holden says he is six foot two in height. That would make him a very tall teenager.

(759) Gary Cooper was an American actor. He was very popular and known for playing heroes.

(760) 'Dolled up' means to get dressed up and make oneself smart and presentable.

(761) Holden is confused over whether or not he likes Sally Hayes. He finds her attractive but annoying. Holden seems to deduce that if he only went out with Sally because he found her attractive he would be as shallow as Stradlater. Holden wants a deeper bond with any romantic partner.

(762) Andover is a town in Massachusetts. It is the home of one of the oldest independent secondary prep schools in America · Phillips Academy.

(763) Holden clearly dislikes the word 'grand'. He thinks it is phony.

(764) Ralph Bakshi's idea for a Catcher movie was to do it

partly animated. Bakshi's animated films include Lord of the Rings and Fritz the Cat. Bakshi was from Brooklyn and identified with Holden Caulfield.

(765) Joyce Maynard said that Salinger was a big fan of the Peter Sellers comedy film The Party.

(766) Ernie is pianist at the club in Greenwich Village. Holden thinks Ernie is a phony because he plays needlessly showy 'ripple' notes and basks in the applause at the end of his set. Holden could be speaking for Salinger here as Salinger hated the sort of ego that Ernie displays.

(767) The fact that Jane is on a date with Stradlater suggests (but doesn't completely confirm) that Jane is a different person now to the one in Holden's memory. Holden is fearful of finding out whether this is the case or not.

(768) Emily Dickinson was an American poet.

(769) The Navajo are a Native American Indian people.

(770) Martin Scorsese's 1976 drama Taxi Driver is often cited as a sort of dark unofficial sequel to Catcher in that Travis Bickle endures an alienating and lonely time in New York and is obsessed with preserving the innocence of a child prostitute he meets. Taxi Driver is considerably darker and more adult than Catcher though. It's hard to imagine that Holden grew up to become Travis Bickle!

(771) Elkdon Hills is Holden's old school. He flunked out of there in the same way that he is flunking out of Pencey. Elkdon is probably no worse or no better than Pencey. Holden's real problem is internal rather than whatever school he is at.

(772) Censorship groups calculated that Catcher had nearly 800 examples of profanity.

(773) Faith Cavendish is the burlesque stripper that Holden tries to call for a date. She is implied to be a girl who likes a 'good time' and maybe even a prostitute - at least that's what Eddie Birdsell suggested. Eddie was the student who gave Holden the number of Faith. Faith doesn't show much interest in a date with Holden though. She prefers her beauty sleep.

(774) JD Salinger would meditate every day after his breakfast.

(775) Where he goes to the Edmont Hotel, Holden gives the driver the address of his parents at first. This could be a simple mistake (he is obviously used to giving his home address to drivers) or could represent a subconscious desire to go home.

(776) The Great Gatsby is, of course, a novel by F. Scott Fitzgerald. Fitzgerald ended his days as a screenwriter in Hollywood. This could be why Holden and Salinger seem to dislike Hollywood. It was rather sad to see a great writer like Fitzgerald as a cog in the Hollywood machine.

(777) Catcher is written partly in a stream-of-consciousness style.

(778) The irony about the rude graffiti Holden finds at the school is that it was probably written by a little kid. The subtext is that Holden's quest to preserve the innocence of children is completely impossible.

(779) 'Lousy with rocks' means to have a lot of jewelry.

(780) Dr Thurmer is the headmaster at Pencey. Holen

especially dislikes Thurmer's description of life as a game where one must abide by the rules.

(781) On reading The Catcher in the Rye for the first time, Joyce Maynard wrote - 'Although this was my first exposure to Salinger's published work, the voice in the novel is instantly recognizable. It could be Jerry talking.'

(782) Matt Salinger said that when he became an actor he kept his family background a secret for as long as possible because he didn't want to feel he was only getting acting jobs because he was JD Salinger's son.

(783) Out of Africa is about a woman named Karen Blixen who protects the African people on her farm. One can see how this has some parallels with Holden's desire to 'catch' and save people.

(784) One of the best books about Salinger is JD Salinger: A Life Raised High by Kenneth Slawenski. Slawenski draws on all these materials (it won't come as a huge surprise to know the Salinger estate did not sanction his book so Slawenski's access to private letters and photographs is virtually non-existent) but tends to concentrate more on Salinger the writer in his younger days than Salinger the eccentric pottering about in the woods in New Hampshire and dabbling with various New Age treatments and theories while he eats raw peas for dinner.

(785) Most of the bad language in Catcher is no worse than what you would hear in a PG-13 film today.

(786) Ring Lardner was known for his sarcasm and humour. This is why Holden likes him.

(787) Mark Chapman read a passage from Catcher in court during his sentencing.

(788) Joyce Maynard said that Catcher and Salinger were a cult at her Yale campus in the early 1970s.

(789) Catcher is about the complexity of the relationship one has with oneself. Holden is confused about who he really is.

(790) Catcher uses free association. Free association is the expression of the content of consciousness.

(791) Strange but true - Matt Salinger once played Captain America in a 1990 film.

(792) Stradlater's shallowness is indicated by the fact that he can't even remember what Jane's name is. He thinks she is called Jean. Jane might be special to Holden but to Stradlater she is just another girl to fumble with in the back of a car.

(793) It has been claimed that the first highball cocktail was brought to America in 1894 by the English actor EJ Ratcliffe.

(794) Although he dislikes Ackley, Holden seems to keep seeking out his company. This is an expression of how alone he feels.

(795) Holden doesn't have much time for organised religion in Catcher. Salinger didn't like big organised structures and felt that people were better off discovering things for themselves as an individual rather than 'recruited' into something.

(796) Phoebe is the only person in the novel who can make Holden happy and lift his mood.

(797) The first Russian language version of Catcher was called Over the Abyss in Rye.

(798) Holden's feeling that society was phony and corrupt anticipated McCarthyism.

(799) Salinger loved the film Casablanca.

(800) It is entirely up to Catcher fans to decide what happened to Holden after the novel ends. It would be nice to think that he gave Jane a buzz.

(801) Salinger did not like trespassers at his Cornish property. There were a few incidents of him coming out with a gun.

(802) Holden often pretends to be someone else in Catcher. This represents his confusion over identity.

(803) When Catcher came out, Salinger was compared to Ring Lardner. This probably would have been flattering to Salinger if he ever read reviews.

(804) Jean Miller said that Salinger was a fan of Judy Garland. He felt there was a purity in child actors because they didn't know how to be arch or pretentious.

(805) In a letter to Jean Miller after Catcher came out, Salinger said his friends were worried that if he moved to Cornish and isolated himself he would have nothing to write about. This sort of came true in the end.

(806) Jean Miller said that Salinger once took her to see the Lunts on stage.

(807) Salinger was Jerry Salinger to his friends and JD Salinger to his readers. It suggests a desire to avoid

becoming too 'familiar' to his readers and separate the artist and person.

(808) Holden is sixteen years old for most of the novel.

(809) Some of those who knew him at Valley Forge, remembered Salinger as being quite snooty and pretentious.

(810) During the war, Salinger wrote a story called The Children's Echelon which featured a scene set at the carousel in Central Park.

(811) Salinger, in contrast to Holden and the headmaster at Pencey, was apparently quite fond of the headmaster at Valley Forge.

(812) Salinger and Jack Kerouac were very nearly classmates at Columbia University.

(813) A portrait of Salinger was put in the Smithsonian when he died. He probably wouldn't have liked that.

(814) Jean Miller said that Salinger had no respect for formal education. He believed learning was done through experience and that regurgitating facts from a textbook was a poor substitute.

(815) When Salinger's story zooey was released, Signet books took out an ad in the New York Times comparing the story to Catcher. Salinger was furious about this as he hated his books to be compared.

(816) It seems that one of the reasons why Sally irritates Holden is that she has an annoying voice!

(817) When he began writing, Salinger was dependent on

selling stories to magazines to make money. This was not easy and he had more than his fair share of rejections.

(818) Salinger could have literally published anything after the success of Catcher. The fact that he published so little suggests he was not interested in money.

(819) Although he was seen as a prophet and guru by his most rabid fans, Salinger never made any public comments about politics or the issues of the day (aside from an article about the justice system in the late 1950s).

(820) Salinger, as you'd expect, got an awful lot of fan mail after Catcher came out. He used to dread going out to his mail box.

(821) Holden decides that he doesn't want to lose his virginity to a bored prostitute who sees him as a financial transaction. He seeks a deeper bond before he is ready to embrace sexuality.

(822) Holden is clearly envious of Stradlater.

(823) Stradlater is the sort of person who can act without introspection or doubt in life. This clearly makes life easier for Stradlater than it is for Holden. Holden would consider himself to have a better moral compass though.

(824) Salinger seemed quite embarrassed by some of the old stories he wrote before Catcher made him famous. It was lucky for him that they were hard to find in later years.

(825) A publisher who briefly dealt with Salinger in the 1990s said Salinger had a bizarre insistence that the title on the spine should read across rather than down · even though this is virtually impossible!

(826) Because he never did interviews, we know surprisingly little of Salinger's own thoughts about Catcher.

(827) The Russian language version of Catcher had Holden buying Russian meatballs rather than a burger.

(828) Someone once tried to sell a toilet that belonged to Salinger for one million dollars.

(829) A teacher once wrote Salinger a long letter about Eastern philosophy. The teacher was bemused when Salinger's reply only concerned itself with the poor quality typewriter ribbon the teacher had used.

(830) Bantam got the paperbark rights to Catcher because Salinger didn't want to renew his contract with Signet. The cover by Avati might have had something to do with this.

(831) After he moved to Cornish, Salinger once wrote a letter in which he said the only thing he liked about New York now was the subway. It's hard to tell if he was joking.

(832) The dialogue between Holden and the cab driver is lauded as some of the best in the book. It has a very New York aura.

(833) Holden is interested in the idea of going to live in a monastery. One could argue that Salinger practically did this himself.

(834) Holden's desire to freeze time could represent his fantasy of eliminating death from the world.

(835) Holden seems especially annoyed when Ossenburger says he prays to God. This feels like Salinger having a dig at mainstream religion.

(836) Holden's cab driver is a lot more concerned about fish than ducks!

(837) The covers for Catcher have used many different colours but red seems to work the best.

(838) Holden seems very young to be having a nervous breakdown and existential crisis. This feels like Salinger writing about his own experience of depression.

(839) In one of the early Caulfield stories, Holden has to face his parents after being expelled. Salinger obviously decided to remove the parents when he used these stories as the basis for Catcher.

(840) Holden's distaste for class divisions and consumerism feels pretty timely today. We now live in a world where class divisions are still pronounced and crooked companies have a monopoly on everything but still try to avoid paying tax.

(841) Despite his disdain for class and wealth, Holden can be snobby. He will notice if someone has a cheap hat or suitcase. This could be termed another contradiction in his character.

(842) A Bulgarian cover for Catcher has an illustration of what appears to be Holden in a raincoat with Phoebe.

(843) There was a champion racehorse named Catcher in the Rye in tribute to the book.

(844) The paperback edition of Catcher was reprinted fifty-two times between 1964 and 1981.

(845) In what could be described as ironic, the enduring

popularity and sales of Catcher were boosted by the loud protests against it.

(846) 'Homey' means nice.

(847) Catcher was said to be tough to translate into Finnish. They didn't really have Finnish words for some of the American slang.

(848) The name Holden is the transferred use of an old English surname. The name is thought to derive from Lancashire. Old English hol 'hollow' + denu 'valley'.

(849) A skate key is a small wrench used to adjust old-fashioned roller skates.

(850) Luce means 'light' in Spanish.

(851) Ackley is an English name. The roots of the Anglo-Saxon name Ackley come from when the family resided in a clearing surrounded by oak trees.

(852) The name Phoebe means 'shining' in its Old English roots.

(853) A Chinese paperback version of Catcher has Salinger's photo on the cover. Salinger would have loathed that.

(854) Allusion is a literary technique where the author references or refers to another work or event.

(855) Holden can't throw the snowball because the purity of the scene is perfect in the snow. Holden doesn't want to alter anything in this precise moment.

(856) 'Hotshot' means someone who is a show-off.

(857) Holden's experience in Catcher can be read as an allegory for youthful ideals meeting the brick wall of adult reality.

(858) James Castle's last name is a reference to his lofty ideals.

(859) A Chinese cover for The Catcher in the Rye once had a photograph of the 1980s teen actor Corey Haim to depict Holden!

(860) Joyce Maynard said Salinger had a long list of foods that were to be avoided because they were supposed to bad for you. His list included, for some reason, tomatoes!

(861) 'Screwball' means someone who is eccentric.

(862) Most Japanese covers for Catcher were quite plain and restrained. Salinger probably would have approved.

(863) A Finnish cover for Catcher had an illustration of a figure in black with a red cap gazing into a blank grey backdrop.

(864) Holden says 'my parents would have about two haemorrhages apiece if I told anything pretty personal about them' this went for Salinger too. He was even nervous about his parents reading Catcher in case they inferred anything personal.

(865) Louis Shaney was a pupil Holden knew at Hooton. Shaney irritated Holden when he seemed, in the middle of a conversation about tennis, to be trying to find out if Holden was a Catholic.

(866) It is not a coincidence that Salinger gave Holden a

last name that ends with 'field'.

(867) Herb Gale is Ackley's unseen roommate.

(868) Salinger didn't like writing long fiction. Even a modest length novel like Catcher was hard work for him.

(869) Holden sells his typewriter to Frederick Woodruff for $20 even though it is worth three or four more times than that. This is another example of Holden not being very good with money.

(870) The bakery near where Salinger lived in Cornish say he liked doughnut holes. Holden has trouble eating doughnuts in Catcher.

(871) Jane is the English form of the Old French name Jehann.

(872) Salinger said he wasn't a born writer. He said he started as a teenager and never stopped.

(873) Sally originated as a pet name for Sarah. Sally means princess or noblewoman.

(874) The name Hayes is derived from name of an Irish god.

(875) Holden never speaks ill of Jane because she is a frozen memory to him that has never been tarnished by adult phoniness.

(876) Sacrilegious is to violate anything that is sacred.

(877) It has been suggested that Salinger chose the name Ackley because it sounds a bit like acne. This sounds like pure speculation.

(878) The origin of the name Caulfield is open to debate. It could be Irish, English, or Scottish.

(879) The actress Mia Sorvino named her son Holden.

(880) Crocked means drunk.

(881) The Catcher in the Rye was part of the school curriculum in British schools for many years.

(882) The name Phoebe is from the Greek phoibus and means radiant.

(883) Holden likes Mercutio in Romeo and Juliet because he is smart and entertaining.

(884) Holden says he is an atheist and fan of Jesus. This is another contradiction.

(885) The snowball Holden doesn't want to throw is symbolic because it will unavoidably melt in the end · just like Holden's childhood.

(886) The Japanese film Weathering With You by Makoto Shinkai has many references to The Catcher in the Rye.

(887) The Finnish version of Catcher is called Sieppari ruispellossa.

(888) Holden doesn't ride the carousel at the end because it represents childhood.

(889) Catcher in the Rye is an influence on the 1994 novel New Orleans Beat.

(890) Mutinying is to revolt or rebel.

(891) Salinger never really made any comment about The Catcher in the Rye being studied in so many schools.

(892) The Catcher in the Rye was required reading in West German secondary schools for many years.

(893) Holden's disdain for money is illustrated by the fact that he often forgets to pick up his change after he has paid for something.

(894) The Catcher in the Rye was mentioned in an episode of the sitcom Archie Bunker.

(896) 'Snappy' means fast.

(897) The ducks are rather like Holden in that they must flee from their problems (the winter).

(898) Grendel is a character in the poem Beowulf.

(899) Joyce Maynard said Salinger was a big fan of the comedy film The Pink Panther.

(900) Joyce Maynard sad that Salinger told her he grew to hate his relatives when he became famous. He said that after Catcher came out some relatives he barely knew suddenly turned up out of the blue.

(901) Critics of Catcher who found Holden miserable and self-indulgent seem to miss the fact that he is self aware when it comes to how melodramatic his introspection is. Holden's humour mitigates his introspection.

(902) Salinger's disenchantment with New York is apparent in Catcher. Salinger would still visit the city but he no longer wanted to live there.

(903) When Holden is wary of going in the museum, one interpretation of this scene is that he doesn't want to be reminded that while the museum is the same he had changed himself.

(904) Joyce Maynard said that Salinger was a big fan of Marlon Brando.

(905) Holden is clearly fascinated by the underbelly of life in New York. He becomes a voyeur at the grotty hotel.

(906) It is bizarre that when he tried to obtain the Catcher rights, Jerry Lewis saw himself playing Holden - despite being in his forties at the time.

(907) The success of Catcher seemed to take Salinger by surprise. No one could have anticipated how successful the book would become.

(908) Some scholars interpret Catcher as a book about sexual abuse. Jane is implied to have been abused or harassed, Holden implies he may have been abused, Stradlater is implied to have taken advantage of girls, and Mr Antolini is implied to have made a pass at Holden.

(909) Salinger conceded to Joyce Maynard that Holdens pack an improbably large amount of stuff into a short time when he is in New York.

(910) Salinger was, unlike Holden, good at History at school.

(911) Holden doesn't really discuss politics in the novel.

(912) One of the reasons why Catcher elicited protests is that it expressed distaste for authority figures.

(913) Although he became quite wealthy through Catcher, Salinger did not live a lavish lifestyle. His house in Cornish was surprisingly modest.

(914) The lack of communication between Holden and his parents is clearly a byproduct of Allie's death. Holden tells us that his mother is still in shock.

(915) It has been argued that Salinger used Catcher as a means to write about his own depression. It was a 'cleansing' experience for him to complete the book.

(916) Believe it or not, the Iranian cover for Catcher is one of the more successful of the foreign attempts at a cover.

(917) Holden's desire in Catcher seems to be to transcend material society. The novel is more complex than the surface story of an alienated boy.

(918) The Catcher in the Rye is mentioned in the John Fowles novel The Collector. The Collector is well worth reading if you've never encountered it.

(919) Holden giving Phoebe his hat is a symbolic moment. He is ready to consider moving on from childhood.

(920) Holden calls his hat a people shooting hat but he doesn't mean this in a literal sense.

(921) Joyce Maynard said that when she lived with Salinger in the early 1970s he rarely spoke about The Catcher in the Rye.

(922) Holden Caulfield is a timeless character. He is the eternal and immortal adolescent and constantly discovered by new generations.

(923) The protests against Catcher in 1951 for promoting homosexuality clearly made a mountain out of a molehill when it came to a possible homoerotic subtext.

(924) Salinger's only company when he finished writing Catcher was his dog.

(925) Salinger's favourite movies included The Thin Man and The Lady Vanishes.

(926) A biopic called Rebel in the Rye was released to indifferent reviews a few years ago. Nicholas Hoult played Salinger. Salinger, were he alive, would have been irritated by such a film.

(927) The East German culture minister tried to suppress Catcher because he thought it might inspire people who wanted to change the political system.

(928) The Catcher in the Rye is mentioned in Woody Allen's film Annie Hall. Alvy Singer is looking for his copy when he breaks up with Diane Keaton's title character.

(929) Despite not publishing anything after the 1960s, Salinger claimed to write every day. It remains to be seen what he actually wrote.

(930) Grand Central Station represents the transient and impermanent nature of life.

(931) In the Salinger story The Ocean is Full of Bowling Balls, the main character Vincent Caulfield has a sister called Phoebe.

(932) Salinger seemed fascinated and perplexed by the enduring interest in him. His silence simply increased the fascination.

(933) Jean Miller said that Salinger owned a beautiful leather bound edition of The Catcher in the Rye.

(934) Salinger's New York was the New York of the 30s and 40s. He was dismayed by changes to the city in later decades.

(935) Holden's crisis is universal in that we all sometimes feel as if the rules and conventions of society are absurd.

(936) Jean Miller said that Salinger despised John Updike. Updike was once critical of Salinger in a review.

(937) Holden's distaste for material possessions or flaunting wealth is displayed when he hates the fact that a pupil has less expensive suitcases than him.

(938) Phoebe writing little detective stories is a nice nod to the fact that Salinger was a short story writer himself.

(939) Phoebe, D.B, and Allie are all depicted as writers but Holden is not.

(940) If one reads Catcher as a war novel, New York is like a battlefield that Holden must survive.

(941) At the end of Catcher, Holden implies he is going back to school but doesn't know if he'll apply himself this time.

(942) Despite his grey hairs and height, Holden seems to have trouble getting an alcoholic drink anywhere.

(943) Salinger was fond of ice-skating in his youth. He includes ice-skating in Catcher.

(944) Holden's hunting hat flouts convention. You couldn't

imagine Holden in a Fedora!

(945) The Catcher in the Rye is light on plot and heavy on introspection.

(946) The 1950s is often depicted as a nostalgic golden decade but it was also a time of McCarthyism, communist witch-hunts, and a darkening Cold War and atomic paranoia.

(947) The Catcher in the Rye seems to imply that the world is getting worse and not better. Capitalism is creating a dog eat dog society.

(948) When Catcher was published there was more of a distinction between cities and the country. The growth of the suburbs was still relatively new.

(949) A strength of Catcher is that the reader (most readers anyway) feels as if Holden is speaking for them.

(950) Phoebe is by far the most important character apart from Holden. She is the person who makes him change.

(951) The message of Catcher, despite its gloomy reputation, is a positive one. Holden is going through a phase that will not last but his quest for enlightenment will be eternal.

(952) The link between the killer Robert John Bardo and Catcher was debatable. A U2 song Bardo was obsessed with was much important at his trial.

(953) The foreign book covers for Catcher that try to depict Holden on the cover are usually the worst.

(954) When he is on the train and meets the mother or

Ernest Morrow, Holden spins all manner of nonsense to amuse himself. Holden's lies are actually generous to Ernest though - which suggests an innate decency to Holden.

(955) Although Catcher made Salinger quite wealthy there isn't much evidence that he splashed money around. He didn't collect art or paintings or have a fleet of luxury cars.

(956) Salinger felt that publishing wasn't the be all and end all and that it was a beautiful thing to just write for your own enjoyment.

(957) If you were being really cynical you could say it was easy for Salinger to have the ethos of writing purely for your own enjoyment because he was already financially secure through the royalties from Catcher.

(958) Those who encountered Salinger down the decades in his agent's office say that he was friendly, polite, and funny.

(959) Salinger's work tends to rely much more on dialogue than descriptive passages. Catcher's first person narrative imbues the novel with a lot of internal dialogue.

(960) Salinger's private life would come under much more scrutiny if he was a public figure today. Throughout his life he sought out romantic and sexual relationships with teenage girls who were decades younger than him.

(961) You could argue that Salinger was way ahead of his time in writing a novel that is essentially about mental health.

(962) Catcher is seen as the grandfather of the alienated teen trope. It will always be the gold standard that others

aspire to.

(963) There is no evidence that Salinger ever had an alternative title for Catcher.

(964) The title of The Catcher in the Rye only makes sense if you have read the novel.

(965) Ackley and Stradlater are polar opposites. One is unpopular and choleric while the other is handsome and popular. Ackley is authentic though (if not in an appealing way) while Stradlater is superficial.

(966) Holden's flounce out of Pencey is a noble gesture in a sense because it came about through his insistence on defending Jane's honour.

(967) Holden's misreading a line in the Burns poem is the crux of his problem. He needs to starting meeting people rather than trying to catch them.

(968) Salinger's disinterest in fame seemed to completely perplex the media. They were used to writers like Mailer and Capote who seemed to enjoy fame.

(969) Catcher being selected as the Book of the Month Club selection summer release in 1951 was a very big deal because this generated publicity.

(970) Salinger, to the surprise (and probably dismay) of his publishers, was irritated when Catcher was selected as the Book of the Month Club selection summer release. Salinger thought this would delay the release of the book and prolong his agony when it came to the publicity junket.

(971) Salinger had not expected to make any money from The Catcher in the Rye.

(972) Whit Burnett, who published some of Salinger's early stories in his literary magazine and was a sort of mentor to Salinger, was rather annoyed when Catcher was a success because he had missed out on publishing a novel that he had encouraged Salinger to write.

(973) Whit Burnett felt he was never given enough credit for helping to launch Salinger's career in the first place.

(974) Salinger's greatest fear was to come across as smug or arrogant. He therefore went to great lengths to avoid giving the impression that he enjoyed any part of Catcher's success.

(975) After writing Catcher, Salinger veered more and more into writing what you might call religious fiction.

(976) Salinger was fond of Herge's Tintin books and would read them with his children.

(977) It is said that, after Catcher was published, Salinger couldn't settle in Manhattan because he was embarrassed by the wealth of the area.

(978) In 1962, Salinger turned down an invitation from the Kennedys to attend a dinner at the White House.

(979) The James Avati cover of Catcher for Signet books was loathed by Salinger but there was nothing he could do about it because they had a contract to do the paperback.

(980) Salinger had spells of writing block after finishing Catcher.

(981) A number of writers were critical of the fiction Salinger released after Catcher. You could argue that they

were incredibly jealous of him.

(982) One of the French covers for Catcher depicts thick swirls of red velvet paint. It sort of works.

(983) Salinger believed the artist should have complete control over every detail of their work. This is why he took over designing the covers of his books.

(984) It is perhaps not a coincidence that Salinger's writing output seemed to decline when he had children.

(985) One of Salinger's favourite films was Lost Horizon.

(986) Joyce Maynard said Salinger hated Ivy League education.

(987) Holden has more in common with Ackley than Stradlater. He would hate to admit this to himself though.

(988) When he moved to Cornish after Catcher came out, people acted as if Salinger had gone to live on the moon but he was only a couple of hours away from New York.

(989) Despite his morose reputation, Salinger loved comedy films. The Marx Brothers, Laurel & Hardy, and W.C Fields were his favourites.

(990) There are a number of occasions in Catcher where Holden goes to telephone someone but doesn't go through with it. This suggests a fear of connection and rejection.

(991) The Catcher in the Rye came to represent nostalgia for a New York that didn't exist anymore.

(992) Salinger was always dismayed when he returned to New York and noticed that a building or club he

remembered was no longer there.

(993) Holden becomes very ill during parts of Catcher. It is a wonder he didn't get pneumonia.

(994) When he has nearly run out of money, Holden skims his last coins in the pond. This indicates that Holden has little interest in money.

(995) The Caulfields appear to have a maid so they must be quite rich.

(996) When Holden describes a film or a play he sometimes gets characters or plot points from different films and plays mixed up. This suggests Holden is an unreliable narrator.

(997) Holden is sometimes bamboozled and confused by his interactions with people in Catcher. This is one of the reasons why the prospect of avoiding them tempts him.

(998) Holden's sarcasm is clearly a defence mechanism.

(999) Phoebe doesn't change much in Catcher. Her role is to show how Holden has changed.

(1000) Salinger is light on description in Catcher. This is deliberate so that we have to paint pictures for ourselves.

www.ingramcontent.com/pod-product-compliance
Lightning Source LLC
Chambersburg PA
CBHW021545290526
45785CB00004BA/1517

* 9 7 8 1 3 8 6 7 7 7 4 8 9 *